The Maya:
Diego de Landa's Account of the Affairs of Yucatán

El Yllmo. Sr. D. Fr. Diego de Landa — natural de Cifuentes
España, Obispo de Yucatán, Siendo Guardian de este
convento de S. Antonio 1557 fabricó el primitivo claustro
Yglesia y Santuario de la Inmaculada Concepción
actual, cuya milagrosa
la más costosa

Diego de Landa's **Account of the Affairs of Yucatán**

THE MAYA

Edited and Translated by **A. R. Pagden**

A Howard Greenfeld Book

J. Philip O'Hara, Inc. • **Chicago**

Text © 1975 by A.R. Pagden

J. Philip O'Hara, Inc. 20 East Huron, Chicago, 60611.
Published simultaneously in Canada by Van Nostrand Reinhold Ltd., Scarborough, Ontario.

LC Number: 70-190752

ISBN: 0-87955-303-0

First Printing B

For my Mother and Father

Account of the Affairs of Yucatán,
taken from the writing of Padre Fray
Diego de Landa of the order of St.
Francis.

Here there is another account of
the affairs of China.[1]

Very little so far has been discovered about the early life of Diego de Landa. He was born in 1524 in Cifuentes, a small town in the Alcarria, to the northeast of Madrid.[1] At the age of sixteen he entered the Franciscan convent of San Juan de los Reyes in Toledo, and in the summer of 1549 went to Yucatán in the company of six or seven[2] other friars led by Nicolas de Albalate. Cogolludo[3] speaks of him not only as a zealous preacher but also as a skilled linguist who simplified and improved Villalpando's original grammar of Yucatec Maya. His abilities seem to have been quickly recognized, for in 1553 we find him as custodian of the monastery of San Antonio at Izamal.[4] From there he extended his missionary activities into eastern Yucatán, traveling, as was the Franciscan habit, on foot and discalceate. In 1551, however, he was recalled from the field to attend an interim chapter held at Mérida in April of that year. After this he appears to have spent some time at the convent at Conkal in the province of Ceh Pech, although by 1556 he was again in residence at Izamal. That same year the general chapter of the Franciscan order merged the separate *custodia* of Yucatán and Guatemala into a single province, independent of that of Santo Evangelio in Mexico, to which they had previously been attached. On November 13, the first chapter of the province elected Landa as its custodian, a post which he occupied until September, 1561, when he was chosen to become the first provincial. Cogolludo[5] depicts him at this period as bold and somewhat overconfident. On one occasion he is said to have marched into an Indian village, called Zitaz, where no white man had been previously and, before the startled gaze of three hundred armed men, to have released the sacrificial victim from the pole to which he had been bound. Intimidated by his courage and aura of sanctity, the Indians "did nothing but gaze on each other in wonder." Shortly after his election a number of incidents occurred which brought him into conflict both with his religious superiors and with the Spanish crown: from that moment on the amount of information about his activities multiplies.[6]

Early in 1562, Landa began a series of investigations into the

11

suspected continuance, among the Indians of the province, of idolatrous practices long since outlawed by the friars. His suspicions that the readiness with which the Maya had embraced the new religion amounted to little more than the addition of the Christian god to an already flourishing pantheon had first been aroused the previous year when Fray Pedro de Ciudad Rodrigo had discovered the recently buried corpse of a child with the marks of crucifixion on the body. Fray Pedro himself considered that these were natural, or miraculous, a view with which Landa—who later accused his co-religious of attempting to shield the Indians from discovery—did not concur.[7] In May, 1562, two Indian boys discovered some idols and a skeleton in a cave near Mani; these they brought to Fray Pedro, who passed the information on to Landa. Alarmed by what promised to be evidence of widespread idolatry, the provincial ordered Fray Pedro to hold an inquiry. During the following months a large number of Indians were questioned and tortured; many of these confessed to possessing idols or to having performed idolatrous rites. The punishments imposed at this time were relatively mild; but the friars were by now convinced that the land to which they had come was another Canaan and, anxious to extirpate all further idolatry, called upon Landa to come in person to Mani and take charge of the proceedings. He arrived in early June and set up an inquisitorial court comprising three other members apart from himself: Pedro de Ciudad Rodrigo, Miguel de la Puebla, and Juan Pizarro. Throughout June this body questioned and tortured hundreds of Indians whose recorded testimonies soon led Landa to the conclusion that the *caciques*,[8] the chieftains, and other Indian headmen were the principal offenders and that the common people (*macequales*), though guilty of error, were to a great extent the victims of their leaders. "Some," he remarked, "[have] destroyed Christianity among the simple people to such a degree that several of these have said that they were never so idolatrous even when they were heathens; and they have given instruction to others, teaching them false doctrines."[9] He immediately arrested some forty

leading Indians, among whom were ten governors and *caciques* of
the Mani area, including Francisco de Montejo Xiu, a member of one
of the oldest and most powerful Indian families of Yucatán, whose
antecedents Landa describes at some length in the *Account*. This
act precipitated some unrest among the Indian population, and at
the end of June Landa turned for assistance to the secular arm: Diego
Quijada, *alcalde mayor*[10] of Yucatán, was called upon to order a
column of Spaniards to Mani. This force was to be composed
largely of those colonists who held *encomiendas*[11] in the area and
whose loyalties therefore might be relied upon. On July 11 Landa
pronounced sentence in most of the cases, and on the following day
held an *auto de fe* where these sentences, which ranged from simple
acts of public penance to long periods of forced labor, were read and
confirmed by Quijada, who, as his *residencia*[12] was to show, by this
act stepped—for the first time—beyond the limits of his legal authority. Thousands of idols collected by the friars during the course of
their investigations, and the disinterred bones of suspected heretics
already deceased, were publicly burned: the entire proceedings then
closed with a solemn mass of penitence. Twenty-five leading
figures, however, whom it was thought impolitic to expose to
public obloquy, were removed to the care of the secular authorities
in Mérida, there to await further trial.[13] The assize now shifted its
attention to the former Indian states of Sotuta and Hocaba-Homun,
where the proceedings at Mani were repeated. Landa presided over
the hearings at Sotuta while those at Hocaba-Homun were left in the
care of Fray Andrés de Bruselas, head of the monastery at Homun.
Again the friars concentrated their attentions on local dignitaries.
Among these was one Lorenzo Cocom[14] (a brother of Juan, or Nachi
Cocom, who gave Landa much of the information for his *Account*), a
cacique of Sotuta who hanged himself as a consequence of these
inquiries. The more prominent offenders were sent to Mérida to
join the victims of the Mani proceedings.

On August 14, 1562, Fray Francisco de Toral reached Mérida.
Toral was appointed bishop of Yucatán in 1560 and consecrated at

Puerto de Santa María in Andalusia in 1562. The first resident bishop of the Peninsula, he was a confirmed moderate in his missionary policies and could not abhor the methods of inquiry—particularly the use of torture—employed by Landa.[15] He took no pains to hide his dislike for the provincial, and exaggerated accounts of his benignity seem to have circulated rapidly among the Indians. Quijada testified in September of 1562 that one Juan Ku of Mani "declared and made public in the aforementioned town and province . . . that the lord bishop had sent for the provincial in order to send him under arrest to Castile and that it was right that everyone should engage in their idolatries and be permitted their idols and other scandalous things against the lord our God."[16]

With the arrival of the bishop, Landa's already questionable authority as ecclesiastical judge terminated, but Toral now found the province divided for and against him. In the one camp were Landa, Quijada, and most of the Franciscans, in the other the *encomenderos*—whose labor force was being seriously threatened by the possibility of open rebellion[17]—some of the lay clergy, and a few of the friars. After a hurried consultation with Quijada, with the clergy, and with representatives of the *cabildo*, or municipal council, of Mérida, Toral reached a compromise: Landa was to be permitted to continue with his inquiries for the time being but was forbidden the use of torture. Landa, however, replied that nothing could be extracted from an Indian without torture and withdrew from the proceedings. He now set out for Mexico to put his case before the *audiencia*.[18] On September 30 he reached Campeche, where Hernán Cortés's son Martín, now marquis of the valley of Oaxaca, detained him in an attempt to bring about an agreement between the two parties. Toral arrived on December 12 and after a heated discussion with Landa, during which a practical demonstration of the efficacy of torture was suggested, the bishop dispatched Francisco de Montejo and Joaquín de Leguízamo, both men of long-standing experience in the colony, to examine the way in which the proceedings had been conducted.[19] Nothing, however, appears to have come of this, and Toral now took personal control of the affair. He proceeded to reexamine some of the Sotuta findings, and to this end dispatched his notary-public, Juan de Magaña, with an interpreter, Juan Bautista de Campo, to the area. Magaña reported that many of the sacrificial victims were said never to have existed, and that a number of witnesses claimed to have made false statements in order to escape torture. But he seems to have had little faith in the validity of his own report. In a letter to Alonso de Zurita, *oidor* of the *audiencia* of Mexico, he confided, "I believe more in what the Provincial did because of the confidence I have in him, for what I did was achieved without force or any other means of persuasion."[20]

Early in September, Toral had commissioned Andrés de Bruselas to reopen the Hocaba-Homun inquiries. The testimonies extracted on this occasion—supposedly without recourse to torture—confirmed the earlier Sotuta findings but produced little to compare with the spectacular results at Mani. The reliability of at least the details of these cases appears to be fairly well-attested; but the mere similarity between the two reports, given that the witnesses in both cases had once followed the old religion, does not prove the continuation of idolatrous practices.[21] Toral, however, seems to have been convinced that cases of idolatry had occurred but not that these justified Landa's use of torture and over hasty *auto de fe*.

The struggle between the bishop and the provincial had now become a focal point for the rival factions within the colony, whose interests were unconnected with the need to averruncate idolatry. As Landa's position became increasingly insecure, Quijada, who had provided him with secular aid and sat in judgment at Mani, began to come under attack from *encomenderos* and ambitious crown officials. In his *residencia*,[22] conducted by the governor Céspedes de Oviedo in 1566, he was accused, among other things, of causing the death of numerous Indians, misappropriation of funds, and immorality. Toral, on the other hand, now found that he enjoyed a wide measure of popularity. His abolition of torture and widely-known opposition to Landa had reduced the threatened unrest among the native population; and he opposed the *alcalde mayor* on other matters relating to Indian affairs, particularly on the issue about the use of native carriers.[23] He was now able to turn his attention to the *caciques* and other headmen whom Landa had incarcerated at Mérida and who were still awaiting trial. The bishop moved slowly, using the full resources of the law, and it was not until January 2, 1563, that the sentences were announced. Although no record now survives of these, they seem, for the most part, to have been mild forms of physical punishment and ecclesiastical censure. The struggle between Landa and Toral now entered its final phase, and both parties set about preparing to defend their cases before the Royal Council of the Indies in Spain.

In January, 1563, Toral drew up a report on Landa's behavior,[24] alleging misuse of authority, corruption, and careless handling of the missionary program. This *probanza*, and a summary of the events surrounding the dispute, was dispatched to Spain with two covering letters[25] to Philip II. Landa prepared his own defense, resigned as provincial, and in order to be able to plead his case in person departed for Spain in March or April of 1563;[26] among the large number of papers which he took with him must have been the notes on Maya customs and beliefs which he later used for the composition of his *Account*.

His arrival in Spain, however, was delayed for almost a year and a half by illness and shipwreck, by which time the council had already had time to consider the accusations made by Toral and was inclined to treat Landa with severity. But the complexities of the case, and the fact that much of it impinged upon the internal affairs of the Franciscan order, led to its being remitted by the council to the provincial of Castile. In the spring of 1565, a group of canon lawyers and theologians[27] gathered to consider the evidence. They did not reach their verdict, however, until January 26, 1569: Landa was acquitted on all charges.

While he remained in Spain Landa stayed first at the convent of Ocaña: later, when his case had been decided, he moved first to

Guadalajara and then to San Juan de los Reyes in Toldeo, where he
was made master of novices. He seems to have gone from there to
the convent at San Antonio de la Cabrera, whose guardian he became and where he remained until the death of Toral in April, 1571,
and his own appointment as bishop of Yucatán. He left Spain in
1572, accompanied by thirty other friars, and reached Campeche in
October, 1573. He occupied the bishopric for seven years, until his
death in Mérida on April 29, 1579.[28]

II

Diego de Landa's *Relación de las cosas de Yucatán* is the most detailed
account of the ancient Maya to have survived from the early colonial period, when some contact with the pre-Hispanic past was
still possible and the processes of cultural dissolution were not yet
far advanced. Together with a handful of "native" writings which,
although they were written in Yucatec Maya, were taken down in the
Latin script long after the Conquest, it constitutes our only written
evidence about what was once a flourishing albeit still primitive
culture.

The *Relación* was composed during Landa's residence in Spain,
probably sometime in 1566, and may have been intended to form
part of his defense during the investigation, which began in 1565,
of his inquisitorial activities, although there is no evidence that it
was ever submitted as such. Its range is too extensive and its tone—
though frequently derisive—too objective for its sole purpose to
have been that of proving the existence of idolatrous practices
among the Yucatec Indians. Jean Genet claims that in its original
form it was intended for publication,[29] but this contention is unlikely since a *relación* was essentially an official report written without regard for style and structured in such a way as to make it unacceptable to the reading public of its day as a piece of formal
historical writing. It seems likely, as we shall see, that the *Relación*

17

was in fact compiled at the behest of the Franciscan order and intended for the instruction of future missionaries.

The methods of inquiry employed by Landa show him to have been more credulous and more biased than those of his near contemporaries, Sahagún and Motolinía,[30] who prepared similar works to his own on the Mexican Indians. His approach, however, was substantially the same as theirs and consisted of collecting written testimonies, oral accounts, and the replies of witnesses to a number of set questions. This method, which owes more to legal practice than to the example of classical historians such as Herodotus,[31] was to be extensively employed in the compilation of the *Relaciones geográficas* of the later part of the century and provided an example that would be followed in all subsequent ethnographical research. How many and how varied these informants were we cannot know. They included the first conquerors of Yucatán, various native chieftains, and representatives of the Xiu, Cocom, and Chel families. Landa only mentions by name one of these, Juan, or Nachi, Cocom,[32] but internal evidence also suggests that he made extensive use of the work of Gaspar Antonio Chi, a Hispanized Indian who contributed to the *Relación de la Ciudad de Mérida* and the accounts of several other towns in that district.[33] Landa also draws on Spanish accounts. He makes three references to Oviedo's *Historia general*[34] and may have seen a report by Tomás López Medel, an *oidor* sent from Guatemala in 1552.[35]

Unfortunately Landa's original manuscript has not survived. The *Relación* we have is an abstract made in the first half of the seventeenth century and now in the possession of the Real Academia de la Historia in Madrid.[36] It is a small quarto volume of sixty-six folios written in three separate italic hands.[37] The first of these, though highly legible, is written with less care than the second. The third is less tidy than either of the other two and may be slightly later. On the evidence of the handwriting alone it is not possible to date the manuscript more closely. The paper has no discernible watermark. The pages are now bound out of sequence in the following order: 18r-45r: 1r-17v: 46r-66v. The present binding is apparently of the eighteenth century, with no other markings on the spine but for the library pressmark. Beneath the main title is another in the same hand which reads, "Here there is another account of the affairs of China" (Esta aquí otra relación de las cosas de la China). This work is, however, not included in the volume, and a thorough examination of the holdings of the Real Academia has failed to bring to light any work on China which might have been the one the compiler had in mind. The fact that such a work was at one time included with Landa's Relación suggests that the manuscript may have formed part of a larger collection of relaciones dealing with the overseas missions. A collection of this kind could well have been compiled for the Franciscan order, which operated in China, rather than for the secular government, which did not; a wide and thorough understanding of native peoples was a prerequisite of the Franciscan missionaries' program.

The inclusion of our work within a larger collection of this type would explain not only the apparently random nature of the material covered but also the copyists' choice of the topics which they drew from the original when compiling the present abstract. It might explain, for instance, the brevity of the remarks concerning Landa's inquisitorial trials and his struggle with Toral—for by the 1600's these would have ceased to be of much significance—and the inclusion of a sermon apparently unrelated to the narrative. The style of the work, the number of incomplete sentences, the frequency with which the syntax becomes obscure and several repetitions suggest, furthermore, that at one stage of its transmission the work was dictated. This may account for the fact that most of the place names have been filled in by the second copyist[38] and that references to numbered chapters and to items presumably found in the original but not included in the abstract have been retained.

The work of the first copyist covers folios 1r.-50r. with interpolations by the second and third hands; from 50r.-58v. the work is entirely in the hand of the second copyist. This section, which includes the sermon mentioned above and the only chapter and paragraph headings to be found in the surviving manuscript, would appear to be a fragment of a separate transcription from the original. Unfortunately only one of these headings is numbered, and as that is only a paragraph and not a chapter, it provides no indication as to the place of the fragment within the entire work nor any indication how long the original might have been. We may conjecture, however, that the chapters *(capítulos)* to which the manuscript refers were not very long. The word *capítulo* indicates only a division dealing with a single subject, and in many *relaciones* these are written in a single paragraph. The Pérez Martínez[39] edition of the Spanish text divides the existing work into fifty-two such divisions, but we may be sure that the original was well over twice this length.

A number of attempts have been made to locate the missing original manuscript, or a complete copy of it, but none has met with any success. A reference to the original in the *Relación de Chun-chuchú*[40] suggests that Landa had a copy with him when he returned to Yucatán in 1573, and that this was in the chapter library at Mérida, probably until the friars were expelled in 1820. A number of later authors may have had access to Landa's work, suggesting the possibility that more than one copy or summary was in circulation during the seventeenth century. Textual parallels with the work of Antonio de Herrera, the chronicler royal of the Indies (1549?-1625), indicates that Herrera may have had such a copy before him while composing his *Historia*.[41] If this were the case, it may be extant among the uncatalogued papers associated with him in the Biblioteca del Palacio (Madrid).

III

The present manuscript was discovered by the Abbé Brasseur de Bourbourg and published by him in 1864, together with a French translation and a number of textual notes.[42] The text is curiously inaccurate—considering the legibility of the manuscript—and comes to an end at folio 49v. with the words: "Here ends Landa's work." The Abbé, confused by the change of hand at this point, no doubt supposed that the remaining folios constituted a separate treatise. The first complete (though by no means reliable) Spanish text was transcribed by Rada y Delgado and published as an appendix to a Spanish translation of Léon Rosny's *Essai sur le déchiffrement de l'écriture hiératique maya* in 1881. Since then the work has been republished a number of times, although none of the available editions is satisfactory. The most accessible is that published by Porrúa with an introduction by Angel María Garibay Kintana.[43] This, however, was based on the Pérez Martínez edition of 1938 and is so full of errors of transcription as to be nearly useless for any serious purpose.

The first English translation was done by William Gates and published by the Maya Society in 1937 under the title *Yucatan before and after the Conquest*. It is a very free and often inaccurate version, illustrated with a large quantity of miscellaneous line drawings and supplemented by a number of documents and a map of the chiefdoms of Yucatán as they may have appeared in 1579. The second English translation provides the text for the heavily annotated edition of Alfred M. Tozzer, which was first published by the Peabody Museum at Harvard in 1941. Tozzer comments on every single issue raised by Landa and many of his notes constitute short essays on individual topics, "for those who wish a general view of Maya life with an emphasis on religion."[44] Many of Tozzer's comments have now been superseded and some of his ideas are known to be erroneous. Nonetheless his work remains a wealthy repository of information which has been carefully presented and extremely well-indexed. The actual translation, for which Tozzer himself was not responsible, was originally made from the French of Brasseur de Bourbourg and corrected with both the Abbé's Spanish text and that of Rada y Delgado; a final revision, this time against the manuscript itself, was then made.[45] The result is a near literal

21

rendering which often makes nonsense in English where the Spanish, although syntactically obscure, is only freely conversational in style. Furthermore, on the evidence of the readings provided in the footnotes, the collation with the manuscript appears to have been rather hasty. It remains, however, in essentials a reliable text as a framework for Tozzer's extended commentary on Maya life and customs.

The stylistic and linguistic characteristics of the *Relación* present serious problems to any translator. The work in its original form was almost certainly dictated and the resulting narrative lacks any formal organization of sense of style. The language is sixteenth-century colloquial Spanish and presents the reader with problems of interpretation similar to those he will find in the works of Santa Teresa. Ellipsis, the omission of part of the phrase or sentence demanded by logic—a characteristic of the spoken language—is frequent; inversions of the logical order of the statement are also common—not for literary effect but because Landa evidently developed his ideas as he dictated. For the same reason much of the material is confusingly disordered. Despite the use of ellipsis, however, the narrative lacks tautness and shows the disjointedness typical of speech patterns. The sentences are often loosely held together by the conjunction "and" and by other conjunctive devices which enabled afterthoughts or details previously omitted by Landa to be added to the sentence. To save time the pronominal forms and the auxiliary verbs are used in a rather vague way so that it is not always possible to discern what the subject of a sentence is. Landa also has the disconcerting habit of employing the same key word in a sentence to refer to two different things. His use of tenses is also highly confusing: Indian customs which continued in practice after the Spanish invasion are usually referred to in the present tense and those which ceased with the invasion in the past. As examples of both types may occur several times within a single paragraph, the effect can be bewildering.

These and many other stylistic features often make it very difficult to understand what Landa is trying to say. In such a situation a translator is inevitably under some temptation to provide the English-speaking reader with a version that tidies up what Landa actually wrote, supplying him instead with a narrative which represents what the author of the *Relación* probably set out to say. But such unscholarly treatment of a prime source for Maya history and ethnology would be plainly unacceptable. Some emendations have proved unavoidable simply because, for the reasons given above, Landa's highly colloquial sixteenth-century Spanish sometimes resists close translation or because what was intelligible to the reader of that time would be unintelligible today. The text was translated directly from the manuscript and the spelling of proper names and the arrangement of material have been retained as they appear in the original. The numbered paragraph headings, however, are intended for the convenience of the reader and do not correspond to anything in the manuscript. The notes have been kept to the minimum and cover only those points raised directly by statements made in the text itself. For a detailed commentary the reader is referred to the Tozzer edition.

I would also like to express my thanks to † Padre José López de Toro, of the Real Academia de la Historia, for the invaluable assistance which he gave to me during the many days I spent in that institution.

I would like to record a special debt of gratitude to Professor P. E. Russell who read through the entire work in manuscript and made many invaluable suggestions.

Notes

1. Both the Pérez Martínez and the Porrúa editions of the Spanish text reprint, rather confusingly, an inquisitorial document dated 1582, (three years after Landa's death) inquiring, as was required by statute, into the family background of one "Diego de Landa a cleric resident in Mérida in Yucatán" who was an applicant for a post as notary to an inquisitorial *comisario* there. This

Landa came from Amurrio (Alava), had been married before he became a secular priest, and, despite the coincidence of names, was obviously not the same person as the author of the *Account*.

2. Cogolludo, *Historia de la provincia de Yucathan*, lib. V, cap. IX, gives the names of six: Alonso de Alvarado, Landa himself, Francisco Navarro, Antonio de Valdemoso, Antonio de Figueras, and Pedro de Noriega. But in a letter from Luis de Villalpando to the king dated July, 1550, the number is given as seven *(Documentos para la historia de Yucatán, vol. I, p. 4).*

3. *Op. cit.*, lib. V, cap. XIV.

4. Marianus, *Gloriosus Franciscus redivivus*, p. 273.

5. *Loc. cit.*

6. The account given here of Landa's inquisitorial proceedings and his struggle with Toral follows, to a great extent, the summary given by Scholes and Roys in *Fray Diego de Landa and the Problem of Idolatry in Yucatán*, pp. 585-604.

7. Scholes and Adams, *Don Diego Quijada, alcalde mayor de Yucatán* (hereinafter cited as Scholes and Adams), vol. 2, p. 422. This work is a collection of most, if not all, of the documents relating to the trials and subsequent disputes.

8. See n. 8 p. 168.

9. Scholes and Adams, vol. I, p. 62.

10. See n. 27 p. 170.

11. See n. 24 p. 169.

12. An inquiry into the activities of a crown official held on completion of his term of office.

13. Scholes and Adams, vol. I, pp. 69-71. Francisco de Montejo Xiu was also charged with having attempted to burn down Mani in order to escape.

14. Scholes and Adams, vol. I, p. 73. He was accused of having sacrificed two boys before idols which he had placed in the church. According to another Indian witness, Diego Te, he also confessed to having made other sacrifices some months earlier at Chichen-Itza.

15. Lizana, *Historia de Yucatán*, f. 67 v., intimates that Toral's dislike of Landa was personal and could be attributed to the influence of the royal treasurer, Pedro Gómez, whom Landa had obliged to pay for damages caused to his (Landa's) monastery. This seems hardly likely: Toral had good ethical reasons for looking on Landa with disfavor.

16. Scholes and Adams, vol. I, pp. 174-175.

17. Hernando Muñoz Zapata testified at Toral's request that he, Zapata, believed that the punishment of the headmen should be carried out as swiftly as

possible and at a time when the harvest had already been collected, and that the common people *(maceguales)* should be pardoned," so that these provinces may be made safe for they have great need of it as Your Most Reverend Lordship is aware" (Scholes and Adams, vol. I, p. 129).

18. See n. 32 p. 170.

19. Martín Cortés's *declaración* is printed in Scholes and Adams, vol. I, pp. 186-187. Toral's commission to Montejo and Leguízamo is on p. 187.

20. Scholes and Adams, vol. I, pp. 182-184.

21. Scholes and Roys, *op cit.*, p. 600, claim that the accuracy of the witnesses when describing native customs serves to validate their conflicting accounts of time, place, and participant; but whereas a knowledge of pre-Hispanic religious rites must have been common to the whole tribe, proof of actual cases of idolatry needed to rest on precisely the kind of evidence about which there was conflict.

22. The *residencia* documents are printed by Scholes and Adams, vol. 2, pp. 193-379.

23. In May, 1564, the *alcalde mayor* complained to the king that the bishop had made common cause with the *encomenderos* over the latter's right to employ Indian carriers. "He says," complained Quijada, "that the Indians will die of hunger if they are not allowed to carry loads and that I am depriving them of the work that they received by carrying loads, from which great hunger and deprivation will follow, and other frivolous reasons without substance" (Scholes and Adams, vol. 2, p. 83).

24. *Probanza hecha a pedimiento del Obispo Fray Francisco de Toral sobre la manera en que Fray Diego de Landa y otros religiosos usaron la jurisdicción eclesiástica en la provincia de Yucatán* (Scholes and Adams, vol. I, pp. 249-289).

25. In one of these, dated Mérida, March 1, 1563, Toral condemns not only Landa but also Quijada: "The present *alcalde mayor* has no aptitude for the post; on the contrary he is the cause of destruction and unrest because he is a slanderer and has committed grave injustices and given cause for great grievances both to the Spaniards and to the Indians" (Scholes and Adams, vol. 2, p. 38).

26. Unbeknown to Landa, a royal decree *(cédula)* had already been sent to Quijada and the *alcalde mayor* of Cozumel ordering the immediate dispatch to Spain not only of Landa himself but also of Pedro de Ciudad Rodrigo, Miguel de la Puebla; and Juan Pizarro (Scholes and Adams, vol. 2, pp. 65-67).

27. Their names are given by Landa p. 63.

28. Cogolludo, *op. cit.*, lib. VI, cap. VII.

29. *Relation des choses de Yucatan*, vol. I, p. 10.

30. See n. n. 22, 38, pp. 169, 171.

31. Herodotus employed methods similar to those used by the Franciscans in America. Herodotus' historical method was a subject much discussed in the sixteenth century and it is at least possible that the debate had come to the ears of Landa and his co-religious. See A. D. Momigliano, "The Place of Herodotus," p. 137, who denies, however, that it is possible to trace any direct influence of the Herodotan method upon sixteenth-century chroniclers.

32. P.

33. *Relacion sobre las costumbres de los indios.* It is given in translation by Tozzer, *Landa's "Relación de las Cosas de Yucatán"* (hereinafter cited as Tozzer), pp. 230-232. The *Relación de Chunchuchu*, the author of which had seen Landa's work, says that the latter was "compiled with the assistance of Gaspar Antonio, a native Indian of the province versed in grammar and the Castilian language" (*Relaciones de Yucatán*, tom. I, p. 153).

34. See n. 54. p. 173.

35. His account has not yet been brought to light, but Juan Bautista Muñoz copied out chapter twenty in its entirety and a partial translation of this is given by Tozzer, pp. 221-229.

36. Signatura B. 68.

37. Jean Genet, *op. cit.*, vol. I, pp. 10-11, dates it 1616 but gives no reason for doing so.

38. The hand of the second copyist appears on ff. 3v.-4r., 4v., 11v., 20v., 21v., 26r., 50r.-58v., the third hand on ff. 11r., 15v.-16r., 16r.-17r.

39. See Bibliography.

40. *Relaciones de Yucatán*, tom. I, pp. 142-153.

41. *Historia general de los hechos de los castellanos.*

42. See Bibliography.

43. See Bibliography.

44. P. ix.

45. *Ibid.*

THE MAYA

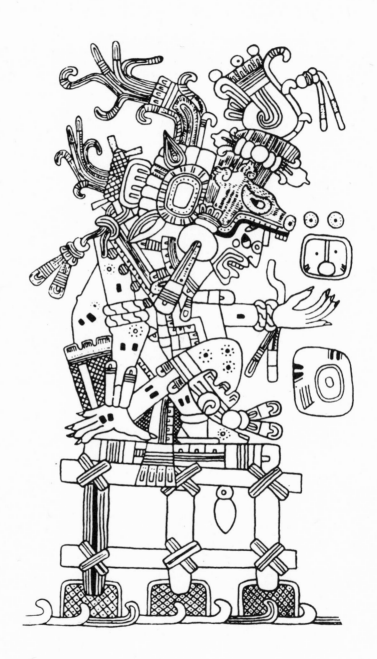

28

Fray Die [go] de Landa:—
MDLXVI

I

Yucatán is not an island nor a point jutting out into the sea, as some have imagined, but a part of the mainland. These people have been misled either by the point of Cape Catoch, which is formed by the sea entering the Bahía de la Ascensión towards Golfo Dulce, and by the point on the other side towards Mexico made by La Desconocida before reaching Campeche, or by the expanse of the lagoons formed by the sea entering Puerto Real and Dos Bocas.

Yucatán is a very flat land, with no mountains, for which reason it cannot be seen from the ships until they are close inshore, except between Campeche and Champoton where there are some low hills forming a headland called Los Diablos.

Coming from Veracruz by way of Cape Catoch, Yucatán lies below 20 degrees [of latitude] and at the mouth of Puerto Real at more than 23 degrees; and from one cape to the other it is at least 130 leagues long in a straight line.

The coast is low, and large ships therefore sail at some distance from the shore.

The coast is strewn with rocks and sharp pieces of slate, which quickly wear away the cables of the ships, but the sea bed is very smooth, for which reason few lives are lost even when the ships are driven onto the shore.

The ebb tide is so great particularly in the bay of Campeche that some places are very often dried up for half a league. Because of these great tides a large quantity of small fish are stranded in the sea wrack, the mud and the pools, and many people live off them.

A small range of mountains crosses Yucatán from one side to the other; this begins close to Champoton and runs as far as the town of Salamanca,[2] which is situated in the opposite corner from Champoton. This range divides Yucatán into two parts: the southern part towards Lacandon and Taiza is uninhabited[3] through lack of water, for there is none except when it rains. The other part, which is in the north, is inhabited.

The land is very hot and the sun burns constantly. There is, however, no lack of cool winds such as those from the northeast and the east which blow steadily there, together with the sea breezes in the evenings.

The people of the country live a long time, and a man of 140 has been found.

The winter begins on Saint Francis's Day and lasts until the end of March, for at that time the north wind blows and gives the people bad colds and fevers because they are scantily dressed.

Towards the end of January and February there is a brief summer with a burning sun; and during this time it only rains when there is a new moon.

The rains begin in April and last until September; and it is at this time that the Indians sow all the crops, which ripen although it never stops raining. They also sow a certain kind of maize which ripens about Saint Francis's [Day] and is harvested very soon after.

In the language of the Indians this province is called *Ulumilcuz* and *Etelceh*, which means "land of turkeys and deer." It is also called Peten, which means "an island," for the natives have been misled by the large number of bays and inlets. When Francisco Hernández de Córdoba[4] reached this land he alighted at the point which he called the cape of Catoch, where he found some Indian fishermen and asked them what country it was. They replied

"Cotoch," which means "our house and our country," and for this reason the point was given that name. When he questioned them further by means of signs about the nature of this land of theirs, they answered "*Ciuthan*," which means "they say so"; the Spaniards therefore called it Yucatán. This was heard from one of the first conquerors, called Blas Hernández, who went with the *adelantado* [Montejo][5] the first time.

In the southern part of Yucatán are the rivers of Taiza and the mountains of Lacandon. Between the south and the west lie the province of Chiapa[s], to reach which one must cross the four rivers that flow down the mountains and join together with others to make the San Pedro y San Pablo, the river that Grijalva[6] discovered in Tabasco. In the west lie Xicalango and Tabasco, which are one and the same province.

Between this province of Tabasco and Yucatán are the two inlets which the sea makes: the larger is a league or more across, but the other is not very wide.

The sea enters the inlets with such fury that it creates a large lagoon which abounds in all manner of fish and is so scattered with islands that the Indians attach signs to the trees to mark out their route when coming or going from Tabasco to Yucatán. These islands and their shores and beaches are filled with such a variety of sea birds that they are a thing of wonder and beauty. There is also a great quantity of game by way of deer, rabbits, the pigs of the land, and monkeys of which there are none in [mainland] Yucatán.

There are an astonishing number of iguanas and on one of the islands is a village called Tixchel.

To the north lies the island of Cuba, with Havana sixty leagues directly opposite, and almost in front of Havana, a small island of Cuba called Pinos.

To the east lies Honduras, and between Honduras and Yucatán there is a very large bay which Grijalva called Bahía de la Ascensión. This is so full of small islands that ships get lost among them, especially those trading between Yucatán and Honduras. Some fifteen years ago a small vessel [*barca*] was lost there with many lives and a large quantity of dry goods. When the ship went down all were drowned except for a person called Majuelas and four others who clung to a section of the ship's mast; and they drifted in this fashion for three or four days unable to reach any of the small islands until their strength gave out and they died, all save Majuelas, who escaped half dead and survived by eating snails and mussels. He crossed over to the mainland from the island on a raft which he made as best he could from the branches of a tree. When he had reached the mainland and was searching the shore for something to eat, he came across a crab which cut his thumb at the first joint and caused him great pain. He then set out along a path through a dense forest in an attempt to reach the town of Salamanca. When night fell he climbed a tree from where he saw a large tiger lying in ambush for a hind. He saw it kill the beast and on the following morning he ate all that remained.

In Yucatán, a little below and in front of the point of Catoch, is Cuzmil, and between the island and the point there is a straight five leagues across which there is a very strong current.

Cuzmil is an island fifteen leagues in length and five across where there are only a few Indians whose language and customs are the same as those of Yucatán; and it lies 20 degrees on this side of the equinoctial line.

The Isla de las Mujeres lies thirteen leagues below the point of Catoch and two leagues from the land in front of Ekab.

It is said that the first Spaniards to reach Yucatán were Gerónimo de Aguilar, a native of Ecija, and his companions who, in the year 1511, at the time of the disturbances in Darien caused by the struggle between Diego de Nicueça and Vasco Núñez de Balboa, followed Valdivia, who set sail in a caravel for Santo Domingo to render an account to the admiral and to the governor[7] of all that had happened and also to take back twenty thousand ducats for the king. On nearing Jamaica this caravel struck some shallows called [Las] Víboras, where she was lost. Only twenty men escaped who, together with

Valdivia, took to a small open boat [*batel*] which had no sails and only poor oars; they remained at sea for thirteen days without any food of any kind. After half their number had died of hunger, they reached the shores of Yucatán in a province that is called Maya, from which the language of Yucatán is called Mayathan, which means "the language of Maya."

II

These poor people fell into the hands of a bad *cacique*[8] who sacrificed Valdivia and four others to his idols and afterwards feasted his people on their bodies. He left Aguilar, Guerrero, and some other five or six to fatten up and they managed to escape and fled into some forests. They reached the land of another lord who was an enemy of the previous one and more merciful; and he made use of them as his slaves; and the one who succeeded this lord also treated the Spaniards with a good grace, but they all perished of disease, leaving only Gerónimo de Aguilar and Gonzalo Guerrero. Of these Aguilar was a good Christian and kept a breviary with which he kept count of the feast days. He was recused by the arrival of the *marqués* Hernando Cortés in the year 1518.[9] Since he understood the language, Guerrero went to Chectemal, which is the Salamanca of Yucatán, and there he was received by a lord named Nachancan, who placed him in command of the affairs of war. He was very skilled at this and many times defeated his master's enemies; he also showed the Indians how to fight, teaching them how to build fortresses and bastions. In this manner, and by behaving like an Indian, he built up a great reputation for himself and they married him to a very high-ranking lady by whom he had children. For this reason he, unlike Aguilar, never made any attempt to escape. On the contrary, he tattooed his body, grew his hair long, and pierced his ears so as to wear earrings like the Indians: and it is possible that he also became an idolater like them.

In the year 1517, during Lent, Francisco Hernández de Córdoba left Santiago de Cuba with three ships to trade for slaves for the mines, as the population in Cuba was much diminished. Others say that he went to discover [new] land and that he took Alaminos[10] with him as pilot and that he reached the Isla de las Mujeres and that it was he who gave it this name because of the idols which he discovered there to the goddesses of that land such as Aixchel, Ixchebeliax, Ixbunic, and Ixbunieta; these were dressed from the waist down and had their breasts covered in the Indian manner. The building was of stone, which astonished them, and there they found some gold objects which they took away with them. They reached the point of Catoch and from there sailed back as far as the bay of Campeche, where they landed on the Sunday of Lazarus, for which reason they called it Lazarus. They were well-received by the lord, although the Indians were astonished by the Spaniards and touched their beards and their persons.

At Campeche they found a building in the sea, close inshore, square and graded on all sides. On top of this was an idol with two ferocious animals devouring its flanks and a long thick serpent of stone which was swallowing a lion; and these [carved] animals were thick with the blood of sacrifices.

At Campeche they learned that close by was a town called Champoton. They found on arrival there that the lord of the place was called Mochcouoh. He was a warlike man who sent his people to attack the Spaniards. This distressed Francisco Hernández, because he could foresee the outcome, but in order not to appear cowardly he also drew up his men and fired off the ships' ordinance. And although the sound, the smoke and the flames of the guns were new to the Indians, they nevertheless attacked with great energy. The Spaniards resisted inflicting numerous severe wounds and killing many; but the lord so urged on his people that they forced the Spaniards to retreat. They killed twenty, wounded fifty and captured two, whom they later sacrificed. Francisco Hernández departed after receiving thirty-three wounds and returned sadly to Cuba, where he announced that the land was very good and rich on account of the gold that he found on the Isla de las Mujeres.

This news moved Diego Velázquez, governor of Cuba, as well as many other people, and he sent his nephew, Juan de Grijalva, with four ships and two hundred men; and with him went Francisco de Montejo, who owned one of the ships; and they left on the first of May, 1518.

They took with them the same pilot Alaminos and reached the island of Cuzmil whence the pilot could see Yucatán. And because on the previous occasion he had sailed along to the right, he now wished to go around to see if Yucatán were an island and so he steered left, following along the bay which is called Ascensión, because the Spaniards had arrived there on Ascension Day. They then turned back along the whole length of the coast until they reached Champoton once again. Here, when they were taking water, the Indians killed one man and wounded fifty, among whom was Grijalva himself, who was struck by two arrows which broke one tooth and half of another. So they departed and called this port, Puerto de la Mala Pelea.[11] On this voyage they discovered New Spain, Panuco, and Tabasco, which took them five months. They wished to land at Champoton, but the Indians prevented them from doing so with great daring coming right up to the caravels in their canoes in order to shoot at them; and so the Spaniards set sail and left them.

When Grijalva returned from his voyage of discovery and trade in Tabasco and Ulúa, the great captain Hernando Cortés was in Cuba, and when he heard the news of so much land and such riches he desired to see them and even to conquer them for God and for his king, for himself and for his friends.

Hernando Cortés left Cuba with eleven ships, the largest of which was one hundred tons, and he appointed eleven captains, he himself being one; and he took five hundred men and some horses and merchandise with which to trade; and he had with him Francisco de Montejo and the above-mentioned pilot Alaminos, chief pilot of the fleet. From his flagship he flew a flag of white and blue flames in honor of Our Lady, whose image together with a crucifix he invariably set up in place of the idols he removed; and on the flag there was a red cross with an inscription which read, *"Amici sequamur crucem, et si nos habuerimus fidem in hoc signo vincemus."*[12]

With his fleet, and with no additional equipment, he set sail and arrived at Cuzmil with ten ships, for one had been separated from him during a storm although he found it later on the coast. He reached Cuzmil from the north and discovered fine stone buildings set up for the idols and a good village. But on seeing so many ships and the soldiers landing, the people fled into the forest.

When the Spaniards reached the village they sacked it and took up lodgings there, and while looking for the people they came across the lord's wife with her children. Through Melchior, the Indian interpreter who had accompanied Francisco Hernández and Grijalva, they understood that she was the lord's wife, and Cortés gave her and her children many presents and sent them to fetch the lord. When he came Cortés treated him very well and gave him certain gifts and returned to him his wife and children together with all the things which the Spaniards had taken in the village. And Cortés asked him to make the Indians return to their homes; and when they had returned he restored to each one everything that belonged to him. Once he had reassured them he preached to them on the vanity of their idols and persuaded them to worship the cross, which he placed in the temples together with an image of Our Lady; and with this public idolatry ceased.

There Cortés discovered that some six suns' journey away lived some bearded men in the power of a lord; and he persuaded the Indians to take a message to them. He found one who was willing to do this, although with great reluctance, for the Indians were afraid of the lord of the bearded men. Cortés then wrote this letter to them:

Honored Sirs, I departed from Cuba with a fleet of eleven ships and five hundred Spaniards and arrived here, on Cuzmil, from where I write you this letter. The people of this island have assured me that in this land there are five or six bearded men who are very like ourselves. They are unable to give me any further description, but from this I believe and am certain that you are Spaniards. I, and these *hidalgos*[13] who have come with me to settle and discover these lands, greatly beseech you to come to us within six days of receiving this, without delay or excuse whatsoever. If you come we shall recognize and be grateful for the good deed that this fleet will receive from you. I dispatch a brigantine for your conveyance and two *naos*[14] for security.

The Indians carried this letter tied in their hair and delivered it to Aguilar, but since they had delayed beyond the allotted time the people in the ships believed them to be dead and returned to the port of Cuzmil. Cortés, seeing that neither the Indians nor the bearded men were coming, set sail on the following day. That day, however, one of the ships sprang a leak and had to return to port. While she was being repaired Aguilar, who had received the letter, crossed the strait between Yucatán and Cuzmil in a canoe; and when the people in the ships caught sight of him they went to see who it was. When Aguilar asked them if they were Christians, and they replied that they were and Spaniards, he cried with delight, and falling on his knees gave thanks to God and asked the Spaniards if it were Wednesday. The Spaniards took him naked as he came to Cortés, who dressed him and was very kind to him. Aguilar then recounted his shipwreck and his hardships and the death of his companions and how it was impossible to send word to Guerrero in so brief a time, for he lived some eighty leagues away.

With the help of Aguilar, who was a very good interpreter, Cortés again preached the worship of the cross and removed the idols from the temple; and they say that Cortés's preaching made such an impression on the people of Cuzmil that they went down onto the shore and called out to the Spaniards who passed that way, "María, María, 'Cortés, Cortés."

Cortés left that place and touched in passing at Campeche but did not stop until he reached Tabasco, where among the other

37

things and Indian women which were given him by the people of Tabasco was a woman who was thereafter called Marina.[15] She came from Xalisco, the daughter of noble parents, and had been abducted as a child and sold in Tabasco. She had been sold again in Xicalango and Champoton, where she learned the language of Yucatán by which she was able to understand Aguilar. In this manner God provided Cortés with good and faithful interpreters[16] by whom he came to have a thorough knowledge of the things of Mexico, for Marina had learned a great deal in conversation with Indian traders and chieftains[17] who spoke constantly of these matters.

III

Some of the old people of Yucatán claim to have heard from their ancestors that this land was settled by people from the east whom God had liberated by cutting twelve paths for them through the sea. If this were true, it must be that all the inhabitants of the Indies are descended from the Jews, for once having crossed the strait of Magellan they must have spread out over more than two thousand leagues of land now governed by Spain.

There is only one language[18] in this country, although on the coast there is some difference in words and in diction, and this has helped greatly with their conversion. The people of the coast are also more refined in their speech and behavior [than those elsewhere], and the women cover their breasts, which the women farther inland do not do.

This land is divided into provinces subject to Spanish towns. The province of Chectemal and Bachalal are subject to Salamanca. The province of Ekab and Cochuah and that of Kupul are subject to Valladolid; those of Ahkinchel and Yzamal, Zututa [Sotuta], Hocabaihumu[n], Tutuxiu, Cehpech, and Chakan are all subject to the city of Mérida. Those of Camol, Campech, Champutun, and Tixchel belong to San Francisco de Campeche.

In Yucatán there are many buildings of great beauty, and these are the most remarkable sight to be seen in the Indies. They are all of finely hewn stone, although nowhere in the land is there metal of any kind wherewith to work it.

The buildings stand very close together and they are temples. The reason for this is that the population has moved a great many times; and in each town where they settled they built a temple on account of the abundance of stone, lime, and a certain kind of white earth which is excellent for building. These buildings were made exclusively by Indians and proof of this may be seen in the naked stone statues, made modest by long girdles which they call in their language ex, and by other devices which the Indians wear.

While this religious, the author of this work, was in that land there was discovered in a building which had been destroyed a large urn which had three handles and was painted on the outside with silver flames; inside were the ashes of a burned body and some bones from the arms and legs, which were wonderfully thick, together with three fine pieces of good stone of the kind which the Indians used for money.

These buildings of Yzamal numbered eleven or twelve in all but no one could remember who had built them; and at the request of the Indians a monastery was established in one of them in 1549 and was called San Antonio.

The next most important buildings are those of Tikoch [Tihoo] and Chicheniza,[19] which will be described later.

Chicheniza is a very fine site, ten leagues from Yzamal and eleven from Valladolid, where they say reigned three lords who were brothers and who had come to the land from the west and who were very pious, for which reason they built very beautiful temples. They lived very modestly without wives,[20] but one died or went away and the others grew self-interested and unjust, and for this reason they were killed.

The decoration of the principal building will be described later, and we will also write about the well where they threw living

39

men and other precious things in sacrifice. This well is more than seven *estados*[21] deep before the water is reached and much more than one hundred feet across. It is cut out from the rock, which is a marvel, and the water is seen to be green, which they say is caused by the trees that surround it.

There is a belief among the Indians that there reigned over the Izaes, who settled in Chicheniza, a great lord called Cuculcan;[22] and this is manifestly true because the main building is called Cuculcan. They say that he came from the west, but they disagree as to whether he came before or after or with the Yzaes. They say that he was very handsome and had neither wife nor children, and that after his return he was regarded in Mexico as one of their gods and called Cezalcouati. In Yucatán they also regarded him as a god because he was a great statesman [*republicano*], and this may be seen in the order that he imposed upon Yucatán after the death of the lords, so as to assuage the strife that their death caused throughout the land.

This Cuculcan founded another city, and arranged with the natural lords of the land that he and they should come and live in it, and that all business matters and other affairs would be brought there. For this he chose a very good site, eight leagues farther inland from where Mérida now stands and fifteen or sixteen from the sea. There the Indians built a very broad wall of dry stone for about an eighth of a league, leaving only two narrow gateways, although the wall was not very high. In the middle of this enclosure they built their temples; and the largest of these, which is like that at Chicheniza, they called Cuculcan. They also built another round one which had four doors, and was unlike any other in the land. There were several other in a group close together. Within this enclosure they built houses for the lords, between whom alone the land was divided, towns being granted to each one in accordance with the antiquity of his line and his personal merits. Cuculcan gave the city a name, not his own as the Yzaes had done in Chicheniza, which means "well of the Yzaes," but he called it

Mayapan,[23] which means "the standard of the Maya" because the language of that country is called Maya. The Indians call the city Ychpa, which means "within the walls."

This Cuculcan lived with those lords for some years in that city, and leaving them in great peace and friendship, he returned by the same route to Mexico, and on the way he stopped at Champoton; and in his memory and to commemorate his departure he built a fine building in the sea after the manner of Chicheniza and at a far stone's throw from the shore; thus did Cuculcan leave a perpetual remembrance in Yucatán.

When Cuculcan had left, the lords agreed that, in order for the government [república] to endure, the chief command should be held by the house of Cocom, as this was the oldest and the most wealthy, and because the man who ruled over it at that time was the most brave. Once this had been done, they arranged that, as there was nothing within the walls but temples and homes for the lords and the high priest, some houses should be built beyond the walls, where they might lodge some people to serve them and where the people from their towns might go when they came to the city on business. Each one of them placed in his house his own majordomo, who carried with him as a sign of office a short thick stick; and he was called *caluac*. This majordomo kept a count of the towns and of the people who ruled over them, and to him notice was sent of what was required in the lord's house by way of fowl, maize, honey, salt, fish, game, clothing, and other items. The *caluac* always went to the lord's house to see what was needed and provided it immediately because his own home was by way of being the office of the lord.

IV

It was customary to seek out the crippled and the blind in the town and to give to them all that they required.

The lords appointed governors to the towns, and if they proved

41

able, confirmed their sons in the office. They charged them with the kindly treatment of the poor, the peace of the town, and the business of maintaining themselves and their lords.

All the lords took care to respect, visit, and entertain Cocom, accompanying him, feasting him, and coming to him with difficult business. And they lived very much at peace with each other and spent much time in the amusements to which they are accustomed, such as dancing, banquets, and hunting.

The people of Yucatán were as diligent in matters of religion as they were in those of government. They had a high priest whom they called *Achkinmai*, and by another name *Ahaucanmai*, which means The Priest Mai or The High Priest Mai. This person was greatly revered by the lords and had no *repartimiento*[24] of Indians, but in addition to the offerings, the lords made him gifts; and all the priests of the town made contributions. He was succeeded in his office by his sons or closest relative, and in this lay the key to their learning; and indeed it was in such matters that these priests worked most, giving advice to the lords and answering their questions. The high priest rarely participated in matters of sacrifice unless they concerned major feasts or important affairs. He provided priests for the towns when they were needed, examined them in the knowledge of their sciences and ceremonies, charged them with all the duties of their office and urged them to be a good example to the people; and he provided them with their books and sent them out. He also looked after the temples as well as teaching Indian sciences and writing books about them.

He also taught the children of the other priests and the second sons of the lords, who were reared for the office from infancy if they showed any inclination to it.

The sciences which they taught were the reckoning of the years, months, and days, and of their feasts and ceremonies; the administration of their sacraments, and of the fateful days and seasons; their manner of divination, and their prophecies, incidents, and cures for sickness, as well as their antiquities and method of reading and writing where by means of their letters and characters they wrote in glyphs which represented the meaning of the writings.

They wrote their books[25] on a large sheet doubled several times. This closed together between two boards which were highly decorated. They wrote on both sides of the sheet in columns, following the folds; and the paper they made from the roots of a tree, giving it a white gloss on which it was easy to write. Some of the principal lords out of diligence had also acquired these sciences, and although they never used them in public, they were held in great esteem for having done so.

V

The Indians say that many people with their lords came into Yucatán from the south, and it seems that they came from Chiapa[s], although the Indians do not know. But this author considers it to be so, because many words and verbal constructions are the same in Chiapa[s] and in Yucatán, and there is much evidence in the part [sic] of Chiapa[s] of places that have been abandoned. They say that these tribes wandered for forty years through the uninhabited regions of Yucatán with no water except when it rained. At the end of that time they reached the mountains which lie slightly in front of the city of Mayapan and ten leagues from it; and there they began to settle and to build fine buildings in many places. The people of Mayapan became very good friends with them, and were glad that they cultivated the land as if they were natives. Thus the people of Tutuxiu submitted to the laws of Mayapan, and they intermarried, and as the lord Xiui of the Tutuxius was such he came to be held in great esteem by all.

VI

These peoples lived so peaceably that there were never any conflicts, neither did they use weapons or bows even for hunting (although nowadays they are excellent archers) but they used only snares and traps with which they caught a great quantity of game. They had a certain means of throwing darts with a stick three fingers in width, grooved to a third of its length and six palms long; and with this and some cords they threw with force and accuracy.

VII

They had laws against delinquents which were rigorously executed; for instance, they handed over adulterers to the offended husband for him to kill by dropping a large stone on his head from a height, or to pardon if he so wished. On the women they inflicted no punishment other than disgrace, which among them was a very serious matter. They also stoned to death anyone who raped a virgin; and they tell of the case of a lord of the Tutuxius who had a brother accused of this crime, and he ordered him to be stoned and afterwards buried beneath a great mound of stones. They say that there was another law before the foundation of this city which demanded that the intestines of an adulterer should be drawn out through his navel.

VIII

The governor Cocom grew covetous of riches, and for this reason negotiated with the people of the garrison which the kings of Mexico had in Tabasco and Cicalango [sic] to hand over the city to them; thus he brought the Mexican people to Mayapan and oppressed the poor and made many slaves. The other lords would have killed him if they had not been afraid of the Mexicans, but the lord of the Tutuxius never consented to this invasion. The people of Yucatán, finding themselves in such a position, learned the skill of arms from the Mexicans; and so they became masters of the bow and arrow, the lance and the ax, and had their shields and tunics made strong with salt and cotton, as well as other equipment for war. They therefore no longer admired the Mexicans nor feared them, but instead paid little attention to them; and they lived in this way for several years.

That Cocom was the first to make slaves, but from this evil followed the knowledge of arms with which they defended themselves so that they should not all become slaves.

Among the successors of the house of Cocomina [sic] there was one who was very proud and emulated the first Cocom; and he made another league with the people of Tabasco and introduced more Mexicans into the city, and began to tyrannize and make slaves of the common people. For this reason the lords joined forces with Tutuxiu, who was a great statesman [republicano] like his forebears, and they agreed to kill Cocom. This they did and they also killed all of his sons except for one who was away, sacked his house and seized his plantations of cacao and other fruit, saying that by so doing they were being paid for what he had taken from them. The disputes between the Cocoms, who claimed to have been driven out unjustly, and the Xiuis, lasted so long that after having been in that city for more than five hundred years, they deserted and abandoned it and each returned to his own country.

According to the calculations of the Indians, it has been some 120 years since the abandonment of Mayapan. In the main square of that city there are seven or eight stones, each ten feet high and rounded on one side, finely carved and inscribed with rows of the glyphs which they used [for writing]; these have been eroded by rain so that they cannot now be read, but they are believed to be an account of the foundation and destruction of that city. There are others like them at Zilan, a coastal town, although these are higher. When the natives were asked what they were they replied that it was a custom to erect one of these stones every twenty years, which is the number they use for counting their ages. But this appears to be without foundation, for if it were true, there would be many more; furthermore, they are not found in any other town except Mayapan and Zilan.

The most important thing that the lords took with them to their own countries when they abandoned Mayapan was the books of their sciences, for the Indians were always very obedient to the advice of the priests; and it is for this reason there are so many temples in those provinces.

When the son of Cocom (the one who had escaped death because he was away trading with the land of Ulúa, which lies beyond the town of Salamanca) heard of the death of his father and the destruction of the city, he returned very quickly and joined his kinsmen and vassals and went to settle in a placed called Tibulon, which means "we have been cheated"; and his people built many towns in those forests. There proceeded many families from these Cocoms and the province where this lord rules is called Zututa.

These lords of Mayapan did not take vengeance on the Mexicans who had assisted Cocom because they had been incited by the governor of the land and were foreigners. They therefore left them in peace, granting them permission to settle in a town set apart for themselves, or else to leave the land; but they were not permitted to marry the natives of that country but only among themselves. They chose to remain in Yucatán rather than return to the lagoons and mosquitoes of Tabasco; and they settled in the province of Canul, which was assigned to them, and there they remained until the second war with the Spaniards.

They say that among the twelve priests of Mayapan was one who was very wise and had only one daughter, whom he married to a young nobleman called Achchel, and she bore children who were called after their father, as is the custom in that country. They say that this priest had given warning of the destruction of that city to his son-in-law, who was well versed in his father-in-law's sciences; and it is also said that he wrote on the broad part of his left arm certain letters which were of great importance and inspired much respect. Having received this favor from his father-in-law, he settled on the coast until at last he came to establish himself with a great many followers at Tikoch. The settlement by these [people, who took the name of] Chel, was of great importance, for they settled the most notable province of Yucatán, which they called the province of Ahkinchel after their own name; and it was in Yzamal that these Chels resided, and their number in Yucatán increased until the arrival of the *adelantado* Montejo.

Between the three houses of these principal lords, who were the Cocoms, the Xiuis, and the Chels, there were great feuds and enmities which continue to this day although they have now become Christians. The Cocoms accused the Xiuis of being foreigners and traitors who had killed their natural lord and stolen his land. The Xiuis said that they were as good as the Cocoms and just as ancient and lordly and that they were not traitors but had liberated their country by killing a tyrant. The Chel said that his lineage was as good as theirs because he was the grandson of the most highly regarded priest in Mayapan, and as for himself he was a greater man than they for he had made himself their equal. On this account there was trouble about food for the Chel who lived on the coast refused to give fish or salt to Cocom, making him go a long way for it, and Cocom would not allow the Chel to have any game or fruit.

For more than twenty years these people had enjoyed health and abundance and they had increased in number until the whole land seemed to be a single town; and it was then that they built the temples in such profusion which may be seen everywhere today; and passing through the forest the sites of wonderfully built houses and buildings may be seen among the trees.

IX

After these years of prosperity, one night in winter at about six in the evening there arose a wind which continued to increase until it became a hurricane of four winds. This wind blew down all the tall trees which killed a great number of every kind of game. It threw down all the high houses, which, as they are made

47

of straw and had fires inside because of the cold, caught fire and burned a large number of people; and any who escaped were broken into pieces by blows from the falling wood. The hurricane lasted until the following day at twelve when they discovered that those who lived in the small houses had escaped among whom were the newlyweds who are accustomed to build cabins (where they live for the first years of their marriage), in front of the houses of their fathers or fathers-in-law. Thus that land lost the name by which it had formerly been known, to wit "the land of deer and turkeys"; and it was now so empty of trees that the ones which are there at present seem all to have been planted at the same time, for they have grown up to be the same height; and looking down on this land from some high places it seems as if all of the forests had been cut off with scissors.

Those who escaped set about building and cultivating the land, and they increased greatly in the sixteen years of health and good seasons that followed, the last of which was the most abundant of them all. But when they were about to gather in the harvest pestilential fevers came upon the whole land. These lasted twenty-four hours and after they had ceased the bodies of the sick swelled up and burst out full of worms. From this plague many people died and a large part of the harvest remained ungathered.

After the plague was over there followed another sixteen good years in which passions and quarrels were renewed, so that 150,000 men died in battle. But after this slaughter they were calmed and made peace and rested for twenty years, at the end of which time they were afflicted by a plague of large pustules which rotted the body with a foul stench so that their limbs fell into pieces within four or five days. It must be more than fifty years since this last plague, and the great killing of the wars was twenty years before that, and the plague of swelling and worms was sixteen years before the wars, and the hurricane was another sixteen before that, and twenty-two or twenty-three after the destruction of Mayapan. According to these calculations, therefore, it is 125 years since that city was destroyed, during which time the people of this land have undergone the above-mentioned calamities and many others besides which followed the arrival of the Spaniards, as a result of wars or through other punishments that God has sent, so that it is now a wonder to find the people that there are, though they are not many.

X

Just as the people of Mexico received signs and prophecies announcing the arrival of the Spaniards and the extinction of their power and religion, so also did the people of Yucatán some years before they were conquered by the *adelantado* Montejo. In the mountains of Mani, which is in the province of Tutuxiu, an Indian called Ahcambal, who held the office of *chilan*, which is the one whose duty it was to proclaim the Devil's answers, told them publicly that they would soon pass under the rule of a foreign people who would preach to them one God and the power of a tree, which in their language is called *vahomche* and means an upright tree with great power against devils.

The successor of the Cocoms, called Don Juan Cocom[26] after he became a Christian, was a man of great repute and very learned in Indian affairs and very wise and versed in their physical world. He was very well-known to the author of this book, Fray Diego de Landa, and told him many things about their history. And he showed him a book which had belonged to his grandfather, son of the Cocom who had been killed at Mayapan. In it was painted a deer, and his grandfather had told him that when great deer (for that is what the Indians called the cows) entered that land, then the worship of the gods would cease; and so this had come to pass for the Spaniards brought large cows with them.

The *adelantado* Francisco de Montejo was a native of Salamanca and crossed to the Indies after the founding of the city of Santo Domingo in the island of Hispaniola, having first spent some time in Seville, where he left a baby son. He came to the city [*sic*] of

Cuba where he earned his living; and he made many friends on account of his goodly disposition among whom were Diego Velázquez, governor of that island, and Hernando Cortés. When the governor decided to send Juan de Grijalva, his nephew, to trade in the land of Yucatán and to discover more land, on account of the news which he had received from Francisco Hernández de Córdoba who had first discovered it to be a rich land, he decided that Montejo should also go with Grijalva. As Montejo was rich, he provided one of the ships and many provisions, and so was among the second [group] of Spaniards to discover Yucatán. When he saw the coast of Yucatán he was taken by a desire to enrich himself there rather than in Cuba, and on perceiving the determination of Hernando Cortés, he followed him with his fortune and in person; and Cortés gave him a ship to command, making him captain of it. In Yucatán they found Gerónimo de Aguilar, from whom Montejo learned about that land and about its affairs. When Cortés reached New Spain, he at once began to settle and the first town was called Veracruz after the device on his banner. Montejo was appointed one of the *alcaldes del Rey*[27] in this town, an office which he discharged ably; and Cortés publicly declared this to be so when he returned there after the journey he made sailing around the coast. This is why he sent him to Spain as one of the procurators of that commonwealth [*república*] of New Spain, and to carry the king's fifth together with an account of the land discovered and of the things that they were beginning to do there.

When Francisco de Montejo reached the court of Castile, the president of the Consejo de Indias was Juan Rodríguez de Fonseca, bishop of Burgos, who had been misinformed about Cortés by Diego Velázquez, who was governor of Cuba but also sought the governorship of New Spain. The greater part of the Consejo was likewise opposed to Cortés's claims, for it seemed that instead of sending monies to the king he was asking for them. And seeing that negotiations were badly carried out, because the emperor was in Flanders, Montejo persisted for seven years from the time of his leaving the Indies, which was in 1519, until he set sail again in 1526. He opposed the president by his perseverance and spoke to Pope Adrian, who was regent,[28] and to the emperor; from which he benefited greatly, and Cortés's business was settled as was right.

While Montejo was at court he negotiated the right to conquer Yucatán for himself, although he could have negotiated other matters; and they gave him the title of *adelantado*. He then came to Seville, taking with him a nephew of his who was thirteen years old and bore his name. In Seville he found his son, aged twenty-eight years, whom he took with him; and he arranged for himself a marriage with a rich widowed lady of Seville and was thus able to collect five hundred men with whom he set sail in three ships. He continued his journey and reached Cuzmil, an island of Yucatán, where the Indians were not alarmed because they had become accustomed to Cortés's Spaniards. There he managed to learn many Indian words so that he could speak to them. From there he sailed to Yucatán and took possession[29] of it, an ensign of his saying, with the flag in his hand, "In the name of God I take possession of this land for God and for the King of Castile."

In this fashion they sailed down the coast, which was well-populated in those days, until they reached a town on the coast called Conil. There the Indians were greatly surprised to see so many horses and men, and informed the whole country of what was happening and waited to see what the purpose of the Spaniards was.

The Indian lord of the province of Chicaca came to the *adelantado* to visit him in peace, and he was well-received. Among his retinue was a man of great strength, who seized a cutlass from the Negro boy who was carrying it behind his master and tried to kill the *adelantado*, but he defended himself until the Spaniards arrived and the disturbance was quieted. They then realized that it was necessary to proceed with caution.

51

The *adelantado* attempted to discover which was the largest settlement, and he learned that it was that of Tikoch, where the lords of the Chels lived, which was farther down the coast in the direction in which the Spaniards were going. The Indians, thinking that they were leaving the land, made no protest nor attempted to hinder their march; and in this way they came to Tikoch, which they found to be a large and better town than they had expected. It was fortunate that the lords of that land were not the Covohes of Champoton, for they were always braver than the Chels, who, with their priestly functions which survive to this day, are not so arrogant as other Indians. Because of this they permitted the *adelantado* to build a town for his people, and for this purpose gave him the site of Chicheniza seven leagues from there; and it is very fine. From there he went and conquered the land, which he did with ease because the people of Ahkinchel did not resist him, and those of Tutuxiu helped him, and with this the rest offered little resistance. In this manner the *adelantado* asked for laborers to build in Chicheniza, and in a short while they had built a town, making the houses of wood and the roofs of certain palm leaves and long straws of the kind the Indians use. Seeing therefore that the Indians served without complaining, he counted up the people of the land, who were numerous, and divided the towns up among the Spaniards; and they say that the least a man had was a *repartimiento* of two or three thousand Indians. Thus Montejo began to organize the natives in the manner they had to serve in that city of his; and this did not much please the Indians, although they did not show it at that time.

The *adelantado* did not colonize in the manner of a man who has enemies,[30] for the place was very far from the sea as regards comings and goings with Mexico or for interference from Spain. The Indians, thinking that it was a harsh thing to serve foreigners in lands where they were themselves lords, began to attack him on all sides. He defended himself with his forces and his men and killed many of them. But every day the Indians acquired reinforcements so that the Spaniards' provisions began to fail, and at last they silently left the town one night, tying a dog to the clapper of a bell and placing on one side a little bread just beyond his reach. On the previous day they had exhausted the Indians with skirmishes so that they should not be able to follow them. In trying to reach the bread, the dog rang the bell and this greatly startled the Indians, who believed that the Spaniards intended to attack them. When they learned the truth they were very angry and decided to follow the Spaniards along every possible route, as they did not know which way the Spaniards had gone. Those who followed the right path caught up with the Spaniards, and shouted after them as at people who were running away. But six horsemen waited for them on flat ground and speared many of them. One of the Indians took hold of a horse by the leg and pulled it down as if it were a sheep. The Spaniards reached Zilan, which was a very beautiful town whose lord was a boy from the Chels and already a Christian and a friend of the Spaniards; and he treated them well. Close by was Tikoch, which, together with all the other towns on the coast, gave obedience to the Chels, and so the Spaniards were left in safety for a few months.

The *adelantado*, seeing that he could not equip himself with supplies from Spain in that place and that if the Indians fell upon him he would be lost, decided to go to Campeche and to Mexico, thus completely abandoning Yucatán. Between Zilan and Campeche there were forty-eight leagues of densely populated country. He informed Vamuxchel, lord of Zilan, of his intentions and Vamuxchel offered to make the road safe for him and to accompany him. The *adelantado* arranged with the uncle of this lord, who was himself lord of Yobain, that he should be given two of his sons who were well-disposed to accompany him. Thus with these boys, who were each other's first cousins, in yokes and the one from Zilan on horseback, the Spaniards arrived safely in Campeche, where they were received in peace. The Chels departed, but while they were returning to their town the one from Zilan fell dead. From there

53

the Spaniards set out for Mexico, where Cortés had assigned a *repartimiento* of Indians for the *adelantado* in his absence.

When the *adelantado* reached Mexico with his son and nephew, his wife, Doña Beatriz de Herrera, whom he had married clandestinely in Seville, arrived in search of him together with a daughter that he had had by her and whose name was Doña Beatriz de Montejo. Some say that he rejected his wife, but Don Antonio de Mendoza, viceroy of New Spain, intervened and afterwards he acknowledged her. The viceroy sent him as governor to Honduras, where he married his daughter to the *licenciado*[31] Alonso Maldonado, president of the Audiencia de los Confines.[32] After some years he was sent to Chiapa[s] whence he sent his son on his authority to Yucatán, and he conquered and pacified it.

This Don Francisco, son of the *adelantado*, was brought up at the court of the Catholic king. He had accompanied his father when the latter returned to the Indies to conquer Yucatán, and from there had traveled with him to Mexico. The viceroy, Don Antonio, and the *Marqués* Don Hernando Cortés thought highly of him, and he went with the *marqués* on his expedition to California. On his return the viceroy appointed him to rule in Tabasco, and he married a lady called Doña Andrea del Castillo, who had come as a girl to Mexico with relations of hers.

After the Spaniards left Yucatán, there was a drought in the land, and because the Indians had squandered their maize during the wars with the Spaniards they were seized by such a great famine that they were reduced to eating the bark of trees, in particular of one they call *cumche*, which is soft and tender inside. On account of this famine, the Xiuis, who are the lords of Mani, decided to make a solemn sacrifice to the idols, taking certain men and women slaves to throw into the well of Chicheniza. To do this they had to pass through the town of the Cocom lords, their arch enemies, but thinking that they would not revive their old enmities at such a time, they sent word to ask if they might be allowed to pass through their land. The Cocoms deceived them with a kind reply but, giving them lodgings all together in one large house, they set it on fire and killed all those who escaped; and on account of this there were great wars. Then the locusts came upon them for the space of five years so that not a green thing was left, and afterwards there followed such a famine that they fell dead by the roadside. Thus when the Spaniards returned they did not recognize the country, although in the four good years after the locusts things had improved somewhat.

This Don Francisco departed for Yucatán by way of the river of Tabasco and entered through the lagoons of Dos Bocas. The first town he encountered was Champoton, whose lord, called Mochkovoli, had inflicted harm on Francisco Hernández and Grijalva. As he was now dead, there was no opposition there; instead the people of this town supported Don Francisco and his people for two years, during which time he was prevented from advancing any further by the great resistance that he encountered. Afterwards he went to Campeche and came to have a close friendship with the people of that town so that with their aid and that of the people of Champoton he completed the conquest. He promised them that they would be repaid by the king for their great fidelity, although up till now the king has not complied with this.

The resistance was not enough to prevent Don Francisco from reaching Tihoo, where the city of Mérida was founded; and leaving the baggage in Mérida, he began to proceed with his conquest, sending captains to various places. Don Francisco sent his cousin Francisco de Montejo to the town of Valladolid to pacify the villages which were somewhat rebellious and to found the town that is there now. In Chectemal he founded the town of Salamanca and he had already founded Campeche. He then arranged for the service of the Indians and the government of the Spaniards until his father the *adelantado* came from Chiapa[s] with his wife and household to govern in his place. He was well-received in Campeche and called the town San Francisco, after his own name, and afterwards he went to the city of Mérida.

The Indians took ill to the yoke of servitude, but the Spaniards had the villages which covered the land well divided up into *repartimientos*. There were, however, no lack of agitators among the Indians, and because of this they were cruelly punished; and this was the cause of a decrease in the number of people. The Spaniards burned alive some of the chieftains of the province of Cupul and hanged others. A charge was brought against the people of Yobain, a town of the Chels. They took the chieftains and placed them in irons inside a house and set fire to the house so that they were all burned in the most inhuman way possible. And this Diego de Landa says that he saw a tree near the town from whose branches a captain hanged many Indian women, and from their feet he also hanged the infant children. In this same town, and in another two leagues away called Verey, they hanged two Indian women, one of whom was a virgin and the other recently married, for no other crime than that they were very beautiful and might cause disturbances within the Spanish camp and also so that the Indians should think that the Spaniards were uninterested in women. These two are well-remembered among the Indians and the Spaniards because of their great beauty and because of the cruelty with which they were killed.

The Indians of the provinces of Cochua and Chectemal rebelled, and the Spaniards pacified them in such a manner that from being the two most settled and populous provinces they became the most desolate in all that land. There the Spaniards committed the most unheard of cruelties; they cut off hands, arms, and legs, and women's breasts; and they threw the Indians into deep lakes and stabbed the children because they could not walk as fast as their mothers. If those whom they had chained together by the neck fell ill, or did not walk as fast as the others, they cut off their heads so as not to have to stop to release them, and with like treatment they took along a large number of men and women captives to serve them. It is said that Don Francisco de Montejo did not commit any of these cruelties, nor was he present at them; on the contrary, they seemed to him to be a wicked thing, but he could do nothing to prevent them.

The Spaniards excused themselves by saying that as they themselves were but few in number they could not subjugate so many people without recourse to terrible punishments. To support this view they brought forward examples from history and from the journey of the Hebrews to the Promised Land when great cruelties were committed by the command of God. On the other hand the Indians had the right to defend their liberty and to trust in their captains, for there were many valiant ones among them and they thought that they would prove so against the Spaniards.

The Indians tell the story of a Spanish crossbowman and an Indian archer, who, as they were both very skilled, attempted to kill each other but were unable to take each other off guard. The Spaniard feigned inattention by placing one knee on the ground and the Indian fired an arrow into his hand, which followed up his arm and split the bones apart, but at the same time the Spaniard released his crossbow and struck the Indian in the chest. As he was mortally wounded, he cut a vine, which is like an osier and very much longer, and hanged himself with it in sight of everyone so that no one should say that a Spaniard had killed him, and there are many examples of such bravery.

Before the Spaniards overran that country, the natives had lived together in towns in a politic fashion and they had kept the land very clean and free from weeds and had planted some very good trees. Their living quarters had been arranged in the following manner: in the middle of the town were the temples with beautiful squares, and around the temples were the houses of the lords and the priests, and after that came those of the chieftains and then, close to them, the homes of the richest and most highly regarded people, while on the confines of the town stood the houses of the poor.[33] Where there were few wells, these were dug close to the houses of the lords; and the lands were planted with wine trees and sown with cotton, pepper, and maize. They lived in these

57

congregations for fear that their enemies would take them captive, but on account of the wars with the Spaniards they were scattered throughout the forests.

The Indians of Valladolid, because of their evil ways and because of their ill-treatment by the Spaniards, conspired to kill the Spaniards when these divided up to collect the tribute; and in one day the Indians killed seventeen Spaniards and four hundred servants of those whom they had killed and of those who remained alive; and they sent some legs and arms through the whole country as a sign of what they had done and to encourage others to revolt. But these others did not wish to do so, and because of this the *adelantado* was able to come to the aid of the Spaniards of Valladolid and to punish the Indians.

The *adelantado* had trouble with the people of Mérida which was exacerbated by a decree from the emperor depriving all the governors of Indians. A receiver went to Yucatán and took his Indians from the *adelantado* and placed them under the crown; after this he [Montejo] submitted to his *residencia*[34] before the Audiencia Real of Mexico, which sent him to the Consejo Real de Indias in Spain,[35] where he died full of days and troubles. He left behind him his wife, Doña Beatriz, who was richer than he was himself when he died, and Don Francisco de Montejo, his son, who had married in Yucatán, and his daughter, Doña Catarina, who was married to the *licenciado* Alonso Maldonado, president of the Audiencias of Honduras, Santo Domingo, and Hispaniola and also Don Juan de Montejo, a Spaniard, and Don Diego, a half-breed whom he had had by an Indian woman.

This Don Francisco, after he had handed over the government to his father the *adelantado*, lived in his house as a private citizen as far as the government was concerned, although he was highly respected, having conquered, divided,[36] and governed that land. He went to Guatemala for his *residencia* and returned home. He had four children; Don Juan de Montejo, who married Doña Isabel, a native of Salamanca, and Doña Beatriz de Montejo, who married a relation, the first cousin of her father, and Doña

Francisca de Montejo, who married Don Carlos de Avellano, a native of Guadalajara. He died of a prolonged illness after having seen them all married.

XI

Fray Jacobo de Testera,[37] a Franciscan, came to Yucatán and began to instruct the sons of the Indians; and the Spanish soldiers wished to use the boys as servants, and worked them so hard that no time was left to them to learn religious doctrine. Moreover, the Spaniards fell out with the friars when the latter reprimanded them for the evil they committed against the Indians; and for this reason Fray Jacobo returned to Mexico, where he died. Afterwards Fray Toribio de Motolinía[38] sent friars from Guatemala, and Fray Martin de Hoja Castro sent more friars from Mexico, and they all settled in Campeche and Mérida by concession of the *adelantado* and of his son Don Francisco. These friars built a monastery in Mérida as has been said, and succeeded in learning the language of that country, which is very difficult. The man who knew it best was Fray Luis de Villalpando, who began to learn it by signs and pebbles;[39] and he reduced it to some kind of grammar and wrote a Christian doctrine in that language. The Spaniards, however, created many hindrances, for they were absolute lords and wished everything to be arranged for their own benefit, as did the Indians, who attempted to retain their idolatry and drunkenness; and it was particularly difficult work as the Indians were scattered throughout the forests.

The Spaniards were distressed to see that the friars were building monasteries, and so they drove the sons of the Indians away from their *repartimientos* in order that they should not learn religious doctrine; and twice they burned down the monastery of Valladolid together with its church, which was made of wood and straw. Things were so bad that the friars were forced to go and live among the Indians. When the Indians of that province rebelled they wrote to the viceroy Don Antonio[40] telling him that they had done so for love for the friars. But the viceroy made inquiries and discovered that at the time of the uprising the friars had not yet reached that province. The Spaniards kept watch on the friars by night, to the scandal of the Indians, and made inquiries into their lives and deprived them of their alms.

When the friars saw the damage that was being done, they sent a religious to the most excellent judge Cerrato, president of the Audiencia of Guatemala, to inform him of everything that was happening. When the latter saw the disorder and un-Christian conduct of the Spaniards, who set no limit on the amount of tribute they raised, and extracted as much as they could without command from the king and furthermore employed the Indians in every kind of personal service, even hiring them to carry loads, he imposed a certain limit of taxation, which, although too high, was yet endurable. He also set down exactly which things belonged to each Indian after he had paid tribute to his *encomendero*,[41] and that everything should not belong absolutely to the Spaniards. But they appealed against this, and through fear of the tax took even more from the Indians than they had done previously. The friars went back to the Audiencia and sent an embassy to Spain and complained so much that the Audiencia of Guatemala sent an *oidor*[42] who taxed the land and abolished personal service and obliged some of the Spaniards to marry and took away from them the houses they owned which were filled with women. This man was the *licenciado* Tomas López,[43] a native of Tendilla. His action made the Spaniards abominate the friars even more, and they spread defamatory libels against them and ceased going to their Masses.

This loathing was the reason why the Indians respected the friars, for they saw all the trouble that the latter had taken without any personal interest and that they had won their freedom for them; and such was the Indians' respect that they did nothing without informing the friars and also took their advice. This gave the Spaniards an excuse to say in envy that the friars had done it in order to govern the Indians and to enjoy the very things of which they themselves had been deprived.

The vices of the Indians were idolatry, divorce, and public drunkenness, and the purchase and sale of slaves; and they came to hate the friars because they made them give up these things. But the people on the Spanish side who gave most trouble to the friars, although they did so furtively, were the priests[44] for they were the people who had lost their offices and the profits to be gained thereby.

The way the friars used to teach religious doctrine to the Indians was to take the children of the lords and chieftains and to send them to live in houses which each town had constructed for its own people to the monasteries;[45] here all the people from the same place lived together and their parents brought them food. With these children they placed only those who came to learn the doctrine and, because of their attendance, many became devout and asked for baptism. Once they had been instructed, the children were diligent in informing the friars about cases of idolatry and drunkenness and in destroying the idols, even if they belonged to their parents; they also urged the divorced women and the orphans to complain to the friars if they had been enslaved. Although they were threatened by their own people, they did not stop because of this, but on the contrary replied that they were doing them an honor because it was for the good of their souls. The *adelantado* and the forces of the king have always provided officials to bring the Indians to the classes on religious doctrine and to punish those who returned to their previous way of life. At first the lords were reluctant to give over their children, thinking that the friars wished to make slaves of them as the Spaniards had done, and they therefore presented them with a number of young slaves in the place of their children; but when they understood the business, they handed them over willingly.

In this manner the young people made so much progress in the school and the other people in the catechism that it was a wonderful thing. The friars learned to read and write in the language of the Indians, which was so successfully reduced to a grammatical art that it could be studied like Latin. It was found that they did not

61

use six of our letters which are: D, F, G, Q, R, and S because they have no need of them, but they must double or add some others in order to represent the many meanings of certain words. Thus *pa* means "to open," and *ppa*, pressing the lips tight together, means "to break." *Tan* is "lime" or "ashes" and *tan*, spoken harshly between the tongue and upper teeth, means "a word" or "to talk," and similarly with other words. Because they had separate characters for these sounds, it was unnecessary to invent new letters for them, but rather to employ Latin ones so that they might be familiar to everyone.

The friars also issued commands to the Indians that they should leave the settlements which they had in the forests and gather as before in good settlements in order that they might learn more easily and so that the religious should not have to endure such hardship. The Indians gave alms at Easter and other feast days to support the friars. They did this at the church through two old Indians who had been appointed for the task. With this they provided all the friars required when they went visiting among them; and they also furnished the church with ornaments.

But after these people had been instructed in religion and the boys had benefited from their studies, as we said, they were perverted by the priests whom they had had at the time of their idolatry, and also by their chieftains, and returned to the worship of their idols and again began to offer them sacrifices, not only of incense, but also of human blood. The friars carried out an investigation into the affair. They asked for the assistance of the *alcalde mayor* and apprehended many and brought them to trial. An *auto* was celebrated in which many were set up on scaffolds with pointed caps on their heads, whipped and shorn while some were made to wear the *sanbenito*[46] for a time. Others, in their sadness and because they had been deceived by the devil, hanged themselves. In general, they all showed sincere repentance and a willingness to be good Christians.

At this time there arrived in Campeche Don Fray Francisco

Toral,[47] a Franciscan and a native of Úbeda, who had spent twenty years in Mexico and came to Yucatán as bishop. On account of the information given him by the Spaniards and the complaints of the Indians, he undid everything the friars had done and ordered the release of the prisoners. This offended the provincial, who decided to go to Spain, after first lodging a complaint in Mexico. When he reached Madrid he was censured by the people of the Consejo de Indias for having usurped the office of bishop and inquisitor. In his defense he referred to the powers that his order exercised in those parts, and which had been conceded by Pope Adrian at the request of the emperor, and to the orders of the Audiencia Real de las Indias that he should be given assistance in accordance with that given to bishops. But the people of the Consejo were only made the more angry by these excuses and decided to send him, together with his papers and those which the bishops had sent against the friars, to Fray Pedro de Bobadilla, provincial of Castile, to whom the king wrote commanding him to examine them and act in accordance with justice. But because this Fray Pedro was ill, he entrusted the conduct of the proceedings to Fray Pedro de Guzmán, a learned man of his own order who was well versed in inquisitorial matters. The opinions of seven learned persons of the kingdom of Toledo were presented; and these were Don Fray Francisco de Medina; Fray Francisco Dorantes, of the order of Saint Francis; the master Fray Alonso de la Cruz, friar of Saint Augustine, who had been in the Indies for thirty years; the licenciado Tomas López who was *oidor* in Guatemala of the new kingdom [of Granada] and had been judge in Yucatán; Don Hurtado, a professor of canon law; Don Mendez, professor of theology, and Don Martinez, [Duns] Scotus professor at Alcalá. They said that the provincial had behaved justly in holding the *auto* and in doing those other things to punish the Indians. When this had been seen by Fray Pedro de Guzmán, he wrote about it at length to the provincial Fray Pedro de Bobadilla.

XII

The Indians of Yucatán deserve the king's favor for many things and for the willingness that they have shown in his service. When he was required in Flanders and the princess Doña Juana, his sister, was governor of the realm, she sent a *cédula* to the Indians asking for aid. An *oidor* of Guatemala took this *cédula* to Yucatán and calling together the lords he commanded the friars to preach to them about the things which they owed his majesty and what he now asked of them. When this discourse was over, two Indians stood up and replied that they well knew how much they were indebted to God for having given them so noble and Christian a king and that it grieved them that they were unable to live in a place where they might serve him personally; therefore he should look and see what he required from their poverty for they would serve him with that and if it were not sufficient they would sell their sons and wives.

The Indians built their houses by covering the roofs with straw, of which they had an abundance and of good quality, or with palm leaves which are suited for this purpose. The roofs have very steep slopes to carry off the rainwater. Afterwards the Indians set up a wall in the middle of the house which divided it in half, and in this wall they cut some doors into the half which they call the back of the house, where they have their beds. They whiten the first half with very fine lime, and the lords have theirs painted with many decorations. This half is for the reception and accommodation of guests, and it has no door but is open along the whole length of the house. In the front the roof comes down very low for protection against heat and rain, and the Indians say that it also gives them control over their enemies from the inner part in time of need. The common people used to build the houses of the lords at their own cost. And because these had no doors they considered it a grave crime to do any evil while in the house of a neighbor.

They have a small door in the rear for the necessary service
and beds made of wands on top of which a small mat is placed; and
on this they sleep covered by their cotton blankets. During the
summer they usually sleep in the whitened part of the house on
one of these mats, especially the men. Outside the house, all the
people did the lord's sowing for him and cultivated and harvested
enough for him and his household; and whenever they went
hunting or fishing, or when it was time to bring in the salt, they
always gave a part to the lord, for they always did these things as a
community. When the lord died, he was succeeded by his elder
son, although his other sons were highly esteemed and attended
and regarded as lords. The other chieftains inferior to the lord
were assisted in all matters according to who they were or to the
favors that had been shown to them by the lord. The priests lived
from their own offices and offerings.

The lords ruled the towns, settling litigations and ordering and
concerting the affairs of their domains [republicas], all of which
they did through the hands of their chieftains, who were well
obeyed and highly respected, especially by the rich to whom they
paid visits. They held court in their houses, usually at night,
where they settled public affairs and other business. If the lords
left their towns, they traveled in a large company, as they also did
whenever they left their homes.

The Indians of Yucatán are a well-built people, tall,[48] robust, and
very strong, although usually they are all bowlegged from infancy,
as their mothers carry them from one place to another seated
astride their hips. They thought it beautiful to be cross-eyed, and
the children were deliberately made so by their mothers who
hanged from their hair a little patch which reached down in
between their eyebrows; whenever they raised their eyes it moved
in front of them and thus they became cross-eyed. They had flat
heads and foreheads, and this was also done to them by their
mothers. From childhood they had their ears pierced for pendants
and much torn in sacrifice. They did not grow beards, and it was

65

said that their mothers burned their faces with hot cloths when they were children so that the hair on these should not grow. Now they do grow beards, although they are very rough ones, like horsehair.

They grew their hair long like women and on top of their heads they burned a space like a large tonsure; thus the lower part grew long and the place of the tonsure remained short; they braided the long part and made a wreath of it about their head leaving the queue to hang behind like a tassel.

All the men but none of the women used mirrors, and to call one another "cuckold" they said that his wife tied a mirror into the hair at the back of his neck.

They washed often, taking no care to cover themselves before the women except what they could cover with their hands. They were fond of sweet smells and for this reason carried bouquets of flowers and odorous herbs, which were very intricate and well-made.

They used to paint their faces and bodies red; this looks very ill on them, but they consider it to be beautiful.

Their clothing consisted of a strip of cloth a hand's breadth across which served them both as breeches and stockings. They wound this several times around the waist so that one of the ends fell down in front and the other behind; and their wives carefully decorated these ends with featherwork. They wore long square cloaks which they tied to their shoulders, and sandals of hemp and dry untanned deerhide but no other clothing besides.

Their principal diet is maize, from which they make various kinds of food and drink; and even when it is drunk [instead of being eaten] it serves them for both food and drink. The Indian women leave the maize to soak overnight in lime and water so that by the morning it is soft and therefore partly prepared; in this fashion the husk and the stalk are separated from the grain. They grind it between stones and, while half-ground, make large balls and loads of it to give to workmen, travelers, and sailors; and these balls last several months, and only become sour [but do not go bad]. From the rest they take a lump and mix it in a bowl made from the shell of a fruit which grows on a tree and by means of which God provided them with vessels. They drunk this substance and eat the rest, and it is tasty and very nutritious. From the most finely ground maize they extract a milk which they thicken over the fire to make into a kind of porridge, which they drink hot in the morning. They throw water on what is left over from the morning and drink it during the day because they are not accustomed to drink water on its own. They also toast and grind the maize and dilute it with a little pepper and cacao, which makes a most refreshing drink.

From the ground maize and cacao they make a foaming drink with which they celebrate their feasts. They extract from cacao a grease which resembles butter, and from this and from the maize they make another drink which is both tasty and highly regarded. They make another drink from the substance of the ground maize when it is raw, which is most refreshing and tasty.

They make bread in a number of ways; and it is a good and healthy bread; but it is bad to eat when cold so the Indian women go to pains to make it twice a day. They have not succeeded in making a flour that can be kneaded like wheat flour, and if, as they sometimes do, they make bread like ours it is worthless.

They make stews of vegetables and the meat of deer and of wild and tame fowl, and also of fish; all of which may be found in large numbers. They also have good provisions, because they now breed the pigs and poultry of Castile.

In the morning they drink the hot drink with peppers, which has been described, and at midday the other cold ones, and at night the stews; and if there is no meat, they make their sauces out of pepper and vegetables. The men were not accustomed to eat with the women; they ate on the floor or, at most, off a mat for a table. They eat well when they have food but when they do not they endure hunger very well and survive on very little. They wash their hands and mouths after eating.

They tattooed their bodies, and the more they did this the more courageous and brave they were considered to be because tattooing was a great torment. It was done in the following way: the tattooist marked out the place that had been chosen with ink and then delicately cut in the pictures, and thus these marks remained on the body in blood and ink. The work was done little by little on account of the great pain it caused and afterwards they were ill because the work used to fester and ooze, but in spite of all this those who did not tattoo themselves were jeered at. They like to appear pleasant and charming and naturally gifted; and now they eat and drink as we do.

Indians were very dissipated by drinking, and this was the cause of many evils. For instance, they killed one another and violated the beds of their neighbors, while the poor women believed that they were welcoming their own husbands; they behaved towards their fathers and mothers as if they were in the homes of their enemies and set fire to their houses and, to add to all this, they ruined themselves in order to get drunk. When the drunkenness was general, and part of the sacrifices, they all contributed to the cost; but when it was private, the host bore the cost with the help of his relations. They made their wine from honey and water and a certain root of a tree which is cultivated for this purpose, with which they make the wine strong and foul-smelling.[49] They ate accompanied by dancing and celebrations, seated by twos and fours, and, after eating, the cupbearers, who did not get drunk, brought some great tubs and the celebrants drank until they were bent over double. The women took great care to bring their drunken husbands home.

They often spend on a banquet everything that they have acquired during many days of trading and bargaining. They conduct these celebrations in two ways; the first, the one followed by the lord and chieftains, obliges each of the guests to hold a similar feast. They give each guest a roasted fowl and a large quantity of bread and cacao drink; and when the feast is over they usually give each other a blanket in which to wrap themselves, a small stool, and the finest of their bowls; and if one of them dies, his household or relations are obliged to pay for the feast. The other way is practiced among relations when their children marry or celebrate the deeds of their ancestors. This does not require repayment, but when a hundred people have invited an Indian to a celebration he has to invite them all in return when next he holds a celebration or his children marry. They form lasting friendships which they preserve by means of these invitations, although they live far apart. During these celebrations their drink was served to them by beautiful women who, after they had handed out the bowl, turned their backs on the person who had taken it until the bowl was empty.

The Indians have very agreeable pastimes. Special reference should be made to the players, who act with such great wit that the Spaniards hire them in order for them to witness the jokes that are made between the Spaniards and their maids or between husband and wife or among themselves about the best and worst kind of service; afterwards they depict these things with much skill and ingenuity. They have small drums which they play with the hand and another kind of drum made of hollow wood which has a heavy sad sound and which they beat with a rather long stick which is padded with the gum from a tree around the end. They have long thin trumpets made of hollow wood with large twisted gourds at the end. They also have another instrument made from a whole tortoise together with its shell but with the flesh removed; and this is beaten with the palm of the hand, producing a sad, lugubrious sound.

They have whistles which are made from the leg bones of deer and from large shells and also reed flutes, and with these instruments they made music for the dancers. They have in particular two dances which are well worth seeing. One is danced with sticks, so they call it *colomche*, which has that meaning. To dance it, a great circle of dancers gathers to the sound of Indian music, which sets the pace for them, and then two of them leave the

69

circle in time to the rhythm. One of these dancers clutches a handful of sticks and dances upright with them, the other dances squatting on his heels. Both move in time with the circle, and the one with the sticks throws them with all his strength at the other who, with great skill, catches them with a small stick. When they have finished throwing they return in rhythm to the circle while others leave to do the same as they have done. There is another dance in which some eight hundred Indians dance with small flags and long war-like steps to music and not one of them is out of time. These dances are very tiring because they do not stop all day long and the dancers are given food and drink there. It is not customary for the men to dance with the women.

The Indians had potters and carpenters, and as these made idols of clay and wood accompanied by many fasts and observances, they earned a great deal. They also had surgeons, or more precisely sorcerers, who cured by means of herbs and numerous superstitions; and this was the case with all other professions. The business which they most favored was to take salt, clothing, and slaves to the regions of Ulúa[50] and Tabasco, and there exchange everything for cacao and stone beads, which they used as money.[51] With this they used to buy slaves or finer and better beads, which the lords wore like jewels during celebrations. They also used for money and jewels other beads made from certain red shells, which they carried about in bags of netting. In the markets they traded in every manner of thing found in that land.[52] They gave credit, and made loans and purchases courteously and without usury. The majority of the people were peasants and those who gathered in the maize and other grains, which they kept in very fine caverns and granaries to sell at the proper time. Their mules and oxen are the people themselves. It is normally the custom for each married man and his wife to sow a measure of four hundred feet called "humvinic," which is measured twenty times along its length and twenty across its breadth with a measuring rod twenty feet long.

The Indians have the good custom of helping each other in all their work at harvest time. Those who have none of their own people to help them join together in groups of twenty, more or less, and together they do the work of all of them, each according to his lot; and they do not stop until everything has been done. At the moment the lands are common, and the first person to occupy them sows them. They sow in many places [at once] so that if one area fails another may replace it. The only thing they do to fertilize the land is to collect the waste, burn it, and then sow it. They cultivate from the middle of January until April and then sow when the rains come. This they do by carrying a small pouch on their shoulders and with a sharpened stick make a hole in the earth in which they place six or seven seeds and then cover the hole again with the same stick. After the rain it is surprising how fast the crops grow. The Indians join up in bands of about fifty for hunting and cook the deer's meat on grills because in that way it does not go bad. When they reach the town they offer their gifts to the lord and distribute the remainder among themselves like friends, and the same is done with the fish.

Whenever they go to pay a visit the Indians always take gifts with them in keeping with their position and the host repays them with another gift. The third parties on such visits speak and listen attentively [moderating their speech] in accordance with the person to whom they are speaking. Despite this, they all address each other in the familiar form, although in the course of their conversation the lesser of the two will carefully repeat the name of the office or rank of the more important, and to help themselves out those who have messages to give often murmur in the back of the throat, which is as much to say "until then" or "so that." The women have little to say and are not accustomed to do business for themselves; for this reason the lords mocked the friars, who listened to rich and poor without distinction.

The offenses which they committed against each other were settled by the lord of the town of the offender, and if this was not done it became an occasion and instrument of further quarrels.

71

If they were from the same town, the case was presented before a judge, who acted as an arbiter. After examining the harm done, he ordered satisfaction to be made, and if he were unable to reach a decision on his own, his friends and relations helped him. Such satisfaction was normally demanded for offenses in which someone was killed by accident, or when a wife or husband hanged himself and the other party might be blamed for having given good reason for such an action, or when someone was the cause of a fire among the houses or arable land, beehives or maize granaries. Other offenses committed with intent were always resolved by blood and blows.

The people of Yucatán are very generous and hospitable, for no one enters their homes without him being given whatever food and drink they may have. During the daytime they offer drinks and in the evening food, and if they do not have any themselves, they go out and ask for it in the neighborhood. And if travelers join them on the roads, they must give something to everyone they meet, although they themselves are thereby left with much less.

XIII

They count by fives up until twenty, by twenties until one hundred, and by hundreds until four hundred, and by four hundreds until eight thousand. They use this count a great deal when trading in cacao. They have other very long counts which may be extended ad infinitum, counting eight thousand twenty times, which makes 160,000, and multiplying the 160,000 by twenty, and thereafter multiplying by twenty until they have reached an uncountable number. They count on the floor or on something flat.

They are very concerned with discovering the origin of their families, especially if they come from some branch of the Mayapan. And they attempt to learn this through the priests (for it is one of the sciences with which they are entrusted) and are very proud of the outstanding men who have been members of their families. The fathers' names are always handed down to the sons but never to the daughters. They always called their sons and daughters after their fathers and mothers, with the name of the father as a proper name and that of the mother as an appellative. In this manner they called the son of Chel and Chan "Na Chan Chel," which means the son of these two. This is the reason why the Indians say that everyone with the same name is related, and is treated as such. For this reason when arriving in an unknown place and in need they at once announce their name, and if there is anyone there with the same name they are immediately taken in and treated with every kindness. Thus no man or woman ever married another of the same name, for among them it was a great infamy. They now call themselves by surnames and other names.

The Indians did not permit their daughters to inherit along with their brothers except out of kindness or good will. They then gave them some part of the whole and divided the rest equally among the brothers with the one who had helped most to increase the value of the property receiving the greater part in compensation for his work. If they were all daughters, the brothers of the father or the nearest relation inherited; and if these were of such an age as to make it unwise to hand over the property to them, it was given to a guardian, who was the nearest relative. This person provided the mother for the maintenance of the children because it was not the custom to leave anything in the possession of the mother, otherwise they took the children away, especially if the guardians were the brothers of the deceased.

These guardians gave the heirs all that had been entrusted to them, and default in this matter was considered to be a grave crime among them and was the cause of many disputes. When they did make it over this was done before the lords and chieftains, who deducted from it the cost of bringing them up. They did not surrender any of the products from the lands, except when these had beehives and some cacao trees, because they said that it was

73

difficult enough just to keep them under cultivation. If when the lord died the sons were not of age and the lord had brothers, the eldest brother or the most able then ruled and instructed the heir in their customs and feasts in preparation for the time when he should become a man. These brothers, even after the heir was fit to rule, commanded all their lives. If the lord had no brothers, the priests and chieftains elected a man sufficient for the task.

Formerly, they used to marry when they were twenty, but now they do so at twelve or thirteen and thus they divorce more readily, as they marry without love and in ignorance of matrimonial life and of the duties of married people; and if their fathers could not persuade them to return to their wives, they looked about for another for them and still others [after the second one]. Men with children abandon their wives with the same ease and with no fear that another might take them to wife or that they themselves might wish to return. But with all this they are very jealous and will not tolerate their wives being unfaithful. And now, seeing that the Spaniards kill their own wives on this account, they have begun to maltreat them and even to kill them. If their children were babies when they divorced their wives, they left them with their mothers; if they were males they went with their father and if females with the mother.

Although divorce was a very common and familiar thing, the old people and those of better customs considered it to be wicked, and there were many who had only one wife and they would never marry one from their father's family who bore their own name because among them this was considered to be a wicked thing, and if anyone married his sisters-in-law, the wife of his brothers, he also was held to be wicked. They contracted matrimony, however, with all other relations on their mother's side, even though these might be first cousins. Fathers took great care at the right time to find for their sons women of standing and condition and if possible from the same place as themselves. It was regarded as a mean thing for them to have to find women for themselves or for a

74

father to arrange marriages for his daughters; in order to fix such arrangements they used bride money and dowries, which were only small sums. The father of the boy gave the monies to the father-in-law, and, besides the dowry, the mother-in-law to be made dresses for the bride and her son. On the day, they gathered in the house of the bride's father, and when the meal had been prepared, the guests and the priests arrived; and with the couple and the fathers-in-law present, the priest sought to assure himself that all was well and that the fathers-in-law had dealt with the affairs properly and everyone was content. Then, that very night, they gave his wife to the young man if he was ready for her. Afterwards they had the meal and the celebrations and thenceforth the son-in-law remained in his father-in-law's house, working five or six years for the said father-in-law; and if he failed to do this, they threw him out of the house. Her mother arranged it that the wife should always provide food for the husband as a sign of marriage. Widowers and widows were united without celebrations or solemnification; and it only required that the man should go to the house of the woman and be admitted and given food for them to be married. From this it arose that couples parted with as much ease as they had come together and men abandoned their women as readily as they had taken up with them. The people of Yucatán never took more than one wife, though it has been discovered in other places that people there have many at once. Sometimes the fathers contract marriage for their children against the moment when they will be of age, and during this time they are treated as fathers-in-law.

XIV

There is no baptism in any part of the Indies except Yucatán, where it is even known by a phrase that means "to be born anew" or "once again," but it is not used except in compound words, thus *caputizihil* means "to be born anew." We have been

75

unable to discover the origin [of their baptismal rite], but it is a thing which has always existed among them and which they hold in such veneration that no one failed to receive it. They so revered this rite that anyone who had sinned and was aware of having done so had to make a declaration to the priest, and so much faith did they have in it that they never in any way repeated the sin. They believed that through it they received a proper disposition to be good after their custom, and a protection against devils and wordly things and hoped by means of it to come to a good life, and to achieve the paradise for which they hoped, where, as in that of Mohammed, they are to be given food and drink. They had, then, their customs in preparation for baptism. The Indian women brought up the children until the age of three. They always used to fasten a small white bead into the hair of the crown on the top of the heads of the young men, and the girls wore a thin cord tied below the loins from which a small pendant shell hung down over their sexual parts. It was considered among them to be a sin and a most wicked thing to take these two things from the girls before baptism, which they always received between the ages of three and twelve; and they never married before baptism. When somebody wished to baptize his child he went to the priest and informed him of his intention. The priest then announced throughout the town the baptism and the day on which it would be performed, which they always took care should not be one of the unlucky ones. This done, the person who was holding the ceremony, who was also the one who made the announcement, chose at his own discretion a chieftain from the town to help him in this business and in the matters pertaining to it. Afterwards it was their custom to choose another four men who were old and honored to assist the priest in the ceremony on the day of the feast; and these they chose together with the priest and at their discretion. In this election, the fathers of all the children that were to be baptized always took part, for the feast was for everyone. Those who were chosen they called *Chacs*. Three days before the feast the fathers of the children and the officials fasted, and abstained from women. On the day, they all gathered in the house of the person who was giving the feast. They took with them all the children to be baptized, whom they placed in order, with the boys on one side and the girls on the other, in the courtyard or square of the house, which they kept clean and scattered with fresh leaves. The girls were placed in the care of an old woman as god-mother and a man took the boys into his charge.

Once this was done, the priest attended to the purification of the dwelling and drove the devil from it. To do this they placed four small stools at the four corners of the courtyard while the four *Chacs* sat with a slack cord passing from one to another so that the children remained herded in the middle, inside the space made by the cord. Afterwards, all the fathers of the children, who had been fasting, had to enter the space by passing over the cord. After this or before, they placed another small stool in the middle where the priest sat with a brazier, a little ground maize, and a little of their incense. The boys and girls then came forward in order, and the priest placed a little ground maize and incense in their hands, which each threw into the brazier, and they all did likewise. When these censings were over they took up the brazier in which these had been performed and the cord with which the *Chacs* had encircled them, and threw into a bowl a little wine and gave it all to an Indian for him to carry beyond the town, warning him not to drink it, nor to look back on his return; and with this they claimed that they had driven out the devil.

When this Indian had gone, they cleaned the courtyard and swept out the leaves of the tree that was there, which is called *Cihom*. They then threw down others from another which they call *copó* and put down some mats while the priest was dressing. Once dressed, he came out in a tunic made of red feathers and decorated with other colored feathers and further large feathers hanging from the borders; and he wore on his head a kind of pointed cap[53] made of the same feathers [as the tunic]; and from beneath the tunic itself a large number of cotton strips reached down to the ground like tails. And he carried a hyssop in his hand, made from a finely carved short stick, but in place of the bristles or hairs of a hyssop were the tails of a [rattle] snake, which were like small bells. And he behaved with no less solemnity than a Pope crowning an emperor, for it was a remarkable thing to see how much dignity they assumed with all this apparatus. The *Chacs* then went to the children and placed on all their heads some white cloths which their mothers had bought for this purpose. They asked the older ones if they had committed any sin or obscene act, and if they had done so, they confessed it and were separated from the others. This done, the priest ordered everyone to be silent and to be seated and began to bless the children with many prayers and to asperge them with his hyssop. He completed his blessing with much gravity and then sat down while the chieftain, whom the fathers of the children had chosen for the feast, rose with a bone which the priest gave him, and went up to the children and threatened each one of them nine times upon the forehead. He then wet them with water from a bowl which he carried in his hand, and, without speaking a word, anointed them on their foreheads and on the features of their faces and between the toes of the feet and the fingers of the hands. This water was made by adding certain flowers and moist cacao to a clear water which they said had been collected from the hollows of trees or the stones of the forest. When this anointing was finished the priest rose and took the white cloths from the heads of the children, together with the others which they had hanging round their shoulders and in which they now gathered up a few feathers from some very beautiful birds and some cacao beans. All of these were then collected by one of the *Chacs*. Then the priest cut off with a stone knife the little bead the boys wore fastened to their heads. After this, the rest of the priest's assistants went with a bunch of flowers and a pipe, which the Indians are wont to suck, and threatened each child nine times with each one of these, and then handed them the flowers to smell and the pipe to suck.

Then they gathered up the gifts which the mothers had brought and gave each child a little of them to eat there, for the gifts were of food. Then they took a large bowl of wine and placing it in the middle of the gifts offered to the gods with devout supplications, begged them to receive that small offering from the children. They then called over another, whom they called *Cayom*, to assist them, and they gave the bowl to him to drink, which he did at a single draught, for they would have considered it a sin if he had paused. This done, the girls were dismissed first, and their mothers removed the cords they had worn around their loins until then, and the little shell which they wore over their secret parts. This was as a license for them to marry when their parents should so wish it. Afterwards they sent away the boys, and once they had gone the parents went over the the pile of small wraps which they had brought, and with their own hands distributed them among the onlookers and the celebrants. This done, they completed the feast by much eating and drinking. They called this feast *Emku*, which means the "Descent of God." After the three days of fast which he had been observing, the person responsible for the feast, who had also borne the cost of it, had to abstain nine further days, and this was strictly done.

XV

The people of Yucatán knew naturally when they were doing wrong, and because they believed that evil and sin were the causes of death, sickness, and afflictions it was customary for them to confess whenever they suffered from these things. In this way, when they were in danger of dying, because of illness or some other thing, they confessed their sins, and if they were neglectful, their closest relatives or friends reminded them. They therefore declared their sins publicly before the priest if he were present and, if not, to their fathers and mothers, the wives to their husbands and the husbands to their wives.

The sins of which they most commonly accused themselves were those of robbery, homicide, weaknesses of the flesh and false witness, and with this they thought themselves saved. And frequently when they escaped death there were quarrels between husband and wife over the calamities which had befallen them and between the people who caused them. The men confessed their weaknesses, except those which they had committed with their slave girls when they had any, for they said that they were permitted to treat their own chattels as they pleased. They did not confess sins of intention, although they held them to be wicked, and in their counsels and preachings advised the avoidance of them.

The most common abstentions which they practiced were from taking salt and pepper in their stews, which was a serious matter for them. They abstained from their wives for the celebration of all their feasts.

They did not marry again for a year after being widowed, so that they should have no knowledge of any man or woman during that time. Those who did not observe this they considered to be of little restraint and believed, because of this, that some harm would befall them.

In some fasts observed during their religious feasts they did not eat meat or have any knowledge of women. They always began the duties of their feasts (and likewise the offices of state) by fasting. Some of these fasts were so long that they lasted three years, and it was a great sin to break them. They were so given over to their idolatrous prayers that in times of need even the women, young boys, and small girls assisted in burning incense and in praying to God to deliver them from evil and to repress the devil who was the cause of it.

Even travelers carried on their journeys incense and a small plate in which to burn it. Thus at night, no matter where they were, they set up three small stones and placed on each a little bit of the incense, and they then placed in front of these another three flat stones on to which they threw the incense, praying to the god whom they call *Ekchuah* to return them safely to their homes. This they did every night until they returned home, where there was always someone who had done the same, and more, for them.

They had a large number of idols and temples that were sumptuous after their own fashion. And in addition to the common temples the lords, priests, and chieftains had oratories and idols at home for their own prayers and private offerings. They held Cuzmil and the well of Chicheniza in the same veneration as we do pilgrimages to Jerusalem and Rome; and they therefore used to visit them and to offer gifts, chiefly to Cuzmil, as we do at the holy places. When they did not go in person they always sent offerings; and those who did go were also accustomed to enter the abandoned temples when they passed by them, and to pray and burn copal.

They had so many idols that even those of their gods were not enough for them, and there was no animal or insect they did not make a statue of; and all of these were made in the likenesses of their gods and goddesses. They had some few idols of stone, and others of wood in small sizes but the majority were of clay. The wooden idols were highly prized, and when inherited were held to be the most valuable part of the inheritance. They had no metal idols, because there is no metal in that country. They were well aware that the idols were their own work, and that they were without life or divinity, but they revered them for what they represented and because they had made them, especially the wooden ones, to the accompaniment of many ceremonies.

The most idolatrous among them were the priests, chilans, magicians and physicians, Chacs and *Nacoms*. The office of the priest was to expound and teach their sciences, to expound their needs and remedies, to preach to them, to compute their feast days, to make sacrifices and to administer their sacraments. The duty of the Chilans was to announce the devils' replies to the people; and they were so highly esteemed by the people that they carried them about on their shoulders. The sorcerers and physicians cured

81

by means of leeches fastened to the place where the sick man was in pain, and they also cast lots to prognosticate matters concerning their own affairs as well as other things. The Chacs were four old men who were always chosen anew on each occasion to help the priest in the proper and perfect performance of the feasts. Nacoms had two main functions. The first, which they performed for life, was not very honorable, and this was to open the breasts of the people whom they sacrificed. The second was to elect a captain for war and other functions. This office they held for three years and it was considered to be very honorable.

They offered sacrifices of their own blood, sometimes cutting pieces from the outer part of their ears which they then left in that state as a sign. At other times they pierced their cheeks or lower lips, sometimes they sacrificed parts of their bodies, and at others they pierced their tongues at a slant through the side, passing through the hole some pieces of straw, which caused them great suffering. At other times they slit the superfluous part of the virile member, leaving it like their ears; and our general historian of the Indies[54] was deceived by this into saying that they circumcised themselves.

At other times they performed a filthy and painful sacrifice. Those who were to participate gathered in the temple and stood in a row, then each made a hole in his virile member at a slant through the side, and once this had been done he passed through it as great a quantity of thread as he could, and in this fashion they were fastened together. They also anointed the devil with the blood from all these parts, and he who offered most blood was considered to be the most brave. Their sons began to concern themselves with such things at an early age, and it was a terrible thing to see how inclined they were to it.

The women did not shed their blood in this fashion, although they were most devout, but they smeared the faces of the devils with the blood of the birds of the air and the animals of the earth and the fish of the sea and any other thing they could obtain, and made offerings of their possessions. They drew the hearts from some animals and offered them; others they sacrificed whole, some alive, others dead, some raw, some cooked, and they also made great offerings of bread and wine, and of all manner of the food and drink they used.

For the performance of these sacrifices they had in the courtyards of the temples some carved, tall beams, upright, and near the staircase of the temple they had a wide, round pedestal, and in the middle of this was a stone five or six palms in height, standing upright and somewhat slender. On the top of the stairs of the temple was another pedestal.[55]

Besides the feasts in solemnification of which they sacrificed [animals], they also commanded the priests or Chilans to sacrifice persons to remedy some misfortune or necessity, and everyone contributed to this, either by giving money to buy slaves [for sacrifice] or, out of devotion, by offering up their own small children, who were much feted until the feast day on which they were to be sacrificed, and carefully guarded so that they should not run away or defile themselves by some carnal sin; and while they processed from village to village with dancing, the priests fasted with the Chilans and officials.

When the day came the people gathered in the courtyard of the temple, and if the victim was to be sacrificed with arrows, they stripped him naked and anointed his body with blue, placing a cap upon his head. When they had come to the place where the devil stood, the people performed a solemn dance around the pole, all carrying arrows and bows, and, still dancing, they tied the victim to the pole, dancing all the while and all watching him. The foul priest in vestments then climbed up, and with an arrow wounded him in the secret parts, be he man or woman, and drew off the blood and anointed the face of the devil with it. He then made a certain signal to the dancers and they, as if dancing, passed swiftly one after another and began to shoot at his heart, which had been marked with a white mark. In this fashion, they turned that point in his chest into a hedgehog of arrows.

If they were to remove his heart, they took him to the court-

83

yard with great ceremony and attended by a large company of people, and, having smeared him with blue and put on his cap, they led him to the round altar, which was the sacrificial stone. After the priests and officials had anointed that stone with the blue color and driven out the devil by purifying the temple, the Chacs seized the poor wretch they were going to sacrifice, and with great speed placed him on his back against the stone and held him by his legs and arms so that they divided him down the middle. This done, the executioner came with a large stone knife and dealt him, with great skill and cruelty, a blow between the ribs on the left-hand side under the nipple. He then plunged his hand in there and seized the heart and, like a raging tiger, drew it out alive and, placing it on a plate, handed it to the priest, who went very hurriedly and anointed the faces of the idols with that fresh blood.

Sometimes they performed this sacrifice on the stone and high altar of the temple and then threw the body, now dead, down the steps of the temple. The officials picked it up at the bottom and flayed it all, save for the feet and hands. Then the priest stripped stark naked, and covered himself with that skin while the others danced with him; and this was a matter of great solemnity for them. They usually buried these sacrificial victims in the courtyard of the temple, otherwise they ate them, dividing the bodies up among the lords and others who were present. The hands and feet and the head were for the priests and officials. And they held these sacrificial victims as saints. If they were slaves captured in war, their lord would carry off the bones to use them as a fetish in their dances as a sign of victory. Sometimes they threw living people into the well at Chicheniza, thinking that they would emerge on the third day, although in fact they never appeared again.

XVI

They have offensive and defensive weapons. The offensive ones were bows and arrows, which they carried in their quivers, with flints or very sharp fish teeth for heads. These they shoot with very great skill and strength. The bows are made of a very fine tawny wood which is wonderfully strong and are more straight than curved. The strings are made from the hemp found in that country. The length of the bow is always a little less than that of its bearer. The arrows are made from very slender reeds which grow in the lagoons and are more than five palms long. They tie to the reed a piece of very slender wood into which the flint is inserted. They did not use poison, nor do they know about it, although there is plenty of it for them to do so. They have small hatchets of a certain metal made in this shape which is fitted to a wooden handle, and it serves them both as a weapon and for working wood. They sharpen them by striking the blade against a stone, for the metal[56] is soft. They also had a small lance, an *estado* in length, whose head was made from strong flint; and they had no other arms but these.

They carried for their defense shields that were made out of reeds that were split and carefully woven; these were round and lined with deerskins. They made jackets of quilted cotton soaked in coarse salt and quilted in two thicknesses or quiltings. These jackets were very strong. Some lords and captains had a sort of wooden helmet, but they were few. The bearers of these arms dressed in feathers and the skins of tigers and lions, and those who had them went to war like that.

They always had two captains, one in perpetuity whose office was hereditary, and another who was elected for three years and with many ceremonies, on the occasion of the feast which they celebrated in the month of *Pax*, which falls on the twelfth of May he was captain of the other groups in war.

This latter they called *Nacom*. During those three years he was not allowed to have knowledge of any woman, not even his own wife, nor to eat meat. The Indians held him in great reverence and gave him fish and iguanas (which are like lizards) to eat. He did not get drunk during this period, and kept on one side in his house the utensils and implements which he required. No woman served him, and he did not have much contact with people. After three years he returned to life as before. These two captains were responsible for war and ordered military affairs, for which purpose they kept in each town a number of people whom they had selected as soldiers, and, when required, these people gathered together with their arms. They called them *Holcans*, and when they were not sufficient they gathered up more people, and divided them up [into groups] among themselves. Then they left the town in great silence, behind a tall flag, and in this manner went to attack their enemies with loud cries and great cruelties when they came upon them unprepared.

Along the roads and passes the enemy placed defenses of sharpened stakes [driven into the ground] and [walls] made of stone. After the victory they removed the jawbones of the dead men and wore them stripped of flesh on their arms. They made great offerings of the spoils they took in their wars, and if they captured any distinguished person, they at once sacrificed him. They did not wish to leave alive anyone who might harm them later. The rest of the people remained captive in the power of the person who had taken them.

These Holcans were not paid, except in time of war, and when there was a war the captains gave them certain monies but only a little because they had to pay these out of their own pocket. But if this was not enough, the village helped with it. The village also gave them their food, and this the women prepared for them. They carried it on their shoulders, for they lacked beasts of burden and thus their wars did not last long. Once the war was over, the soldiers caused many disturbances in their villages while the smell of war lasted, and they made the people serve and feast them. And if anyone had killed some captain or lord, he was most honored and feasted.

XVII

86   These people have maintained since their days in Mayapan the

custom of punishing adulterers in this fashion. Once the inquiry has been made and someone convicted of adultery the chieftains gathered in the house of the lord; and when the adulterer was brought they bound him to a pole and handed him over to the husband of the delinquent woman. If he forgave him, he was free; if not, he killed him by dropping a large stone on his head from a high place. The disgrace, which was great, was considered to be sufficient punishment for the wife, and for this their husbands usually left them. The punishment for homicide, even if it were accidental, was death at the hands of the dead man's relatives or otherwise blood money. They paid for, and punished, theft, even if it were small, by making a slave of the thief. It was for this reason that they enslaved so many, especially in time of famine; and this was also the reason why we, the friars, worked so hard to baptize them so that they might be given their freedom. If they were lords or chieftains, the people of the town gathered, and having caught the criminal, they tattooed his face from chin to forehead on both sides as a punishment, for they held this to be a great disgrace.

The young people greatly revered the old and took their advice, and these then boasted of being old and told the young men what they had seen and how they must believe [what they told them]. If the young people accepted the advice of the old, they were given credit for this. The old were so highly esteemed that the young people had no dealings with them except when such contact was unavoidable, and then only if the young people were unmarried, but if they were married hardly at all. Because of this, they usually had in each town a large house whitened with lime, open on all sides, where the young men gathered for their amusements. They played ball and a game with some beans like dice, and many others. They all almost always slept here together until they married.

Although I have heard that in other parts of the Indies they practiced the nefarious sin [of sodomy] in such houses, I have not heard of them doing so in this country, nor do I believe that they ever did it, for they say that those who do are afflicted by this pestilential

87

infirmity are not partial to women, and these people were, for they brought into these places the evil public women, and made use of them there. The poor girls who happened to pursue this business among these people, although they received recompense from them, were harassed to death, so many were the young men who flocked to them. The Indians painted themselves black until they married, and were not accustomed to tattoo themselves except a little until after their marriage. In other matters they always accompanied their parents and so became as great idolaters as they and served them a great deal in their labors.

Indian women brought up their children with all the harshness and nakedness you can imagine. For four or five days after the child's birth they laid him stretched out on a small bed made of wands and there, with his face up, they placed his head between two boards, one at the back of the head, and the other on the forehead, between which they pressed it very tightly and held him suffering there until the head remained flat and moulded, which happened after a few days. Such was the misery and danger to the poor children that some were in peril of their lives, for the author saw one whose skull had been opened behind the ears; and so it must have been with many of them.

They brought them up naked, except that at the age of four or five they gave them a small wrap in which to sleep, and some small strips of cloth to make them decent like their fathers. At the same time they began to cover the girls from the waist down. They breast-feed them for a long time, for they give suck for as long as they are able, and this goes on until the children are three or four years old. This is why there are so many people of great strength among them.

For the first two years they grew up wonderfully pretty and fat. Afterwards, with the continuous bathing given them by their mothers and the heat of the sun, they become dark. But throughout their entire childhood they were pretty and lively and always carried bows and arrows and played with one another. They were brought up in this way until they began to follow the way of life of young people and to hold themselves more highly and to abandon those childish things.

XVIII

The Indian women of Yucatán are generally better-looking than the Spanish women, and bigger and well-built, but not so large-thighed as Negresses. Those who are beautiful pride themselves on it and in a way they are not ugly. They are not white, but rather of a dark color caused more by the sun and continual bathing than by nature itself. They do not make up their faces like our people, for they hold this to be improper. They had the custom of filing their teeth, which made them like the teeth of a saw, and this they considered to be becoming. The task was performed by some old women who filed them using certain stones and water.

They pierced their noses through the cartilage which divides the nostrils down the middle, and placed in the hole a piece of amber; and this was considered an adornment. They pierced their ears in order to wear earrings after the same fashion as their husbands. They tattooed their bodies from the waist up—but they left the breasts free, so as to be able to give suck—in designs more delicate and beautiful than those of the men. They wash frequently in cold water like the men, but they did not do this with overmuch modesty, for they stripped themselves naked in the well where they went to get water for this purpose. They would also bathe in hot water (heated by fire); but this was seldom done and when it was the causes were reasons of health than of cleanliness.

They were accustomed to rub themselves, like their husbands, with a certain red ointment, and, those who could afford it, covered themselves with a certain preparation made from a sweet smelling and very sticky gum which I believe is liquid amber, and which in their language is called *iztahte*. They smeared this on a certain cake resembling soap, and decorated with graceful designs,

89

and with it rubbed their breasts and arms and shoulders, and became, in their opinion, attractive and sweet-smelling. It lasted them a long time without fading away, so good was the quality of the ointment.

They wear their hair very long, and make of this a very graceful coiffure, parting it into two and also plaiting it to achieve another style of headdress. The careful mothers of the unmarried girls usually take such care of their daughters' hair that I have seen many Indian women whose hair is as well-kept as that of a careful Spanish woman. They dress the hair of the girls, until they are grown up, in four plaits and in two, which is most becoming to them.

The Indian women of the coast and of the provinces of Bacalar and Campeche are very modest in their dress because, in addition to the covering they wear from the waist down, they also covered their breasts, securing them up from beneath the armpits with a folded wrap. All the others wore a single garment like a long white tunic open on both sides and drawn into the hips, where it is tied with a width of the same material. They had no other clothes except for the wrap in which they always slept. But when they went on a journey they were accustomed to carry a blanket doubled over or rolled up; and thus they traveled.

XIX

They prided themselves on being good, and they had good cause for so doing because, if we are to believe the complaints made today by the old men, they were wonderfully good before they came to know our people; and of this I will give examples. The captain Alonso López de Avila, brother-in-law of the *adelantado* Montejo, captured, during the war in Bacalan, a young Indian girl who was a beautiful and charming woman. She had promised her husband, fearful lest they should kill him in the war, not to have relations with any other man but him, and so no persuasion was sufficient to prevent her from taking her own life in order to avoid being defiled by another man; and because of this they had her killed with the dogs.[57]

An Indian woman about to be baptized complained to me about a baptized Indian who was enamored of her, for she was beautiful. He waited until her husband was away and went one night to her house, and after having declared his intentions with many flattering remarks but without success, he attempted to give her presents which he had bought for that purpose, and when these did not achieve anything, he attempted to rape her, and although he was a large man, and struggled all night long to accomplish his purpose, he achieved nothing with her except to make her so angry that she came to me to complain of the Indian's viciousness; and what she told me was true.

They are accustomed to turn their backs on the men if they meet them anywhere and allow them room to pass; and they did the same when they gave them drink until they had finished drinking. They teach their daughters all they know, and bring them up well in their fashion, for they scold them, instruct them, and make them work, and if they commit any fault they punish them by pinching them on the ears and arms. If they see them lift up their eyes, they scold them greatly and rub their eyes with their pepper, which is very painful. If they are not chaste, they beat them and rub pepper on another part of their bodies, which is as a punishment and a humiliation. They say of undisciplined girls, by way of a great reproach and a severe reprimand, that they are like women brought up without a mother. They are jealous, and some so much so that they would lay hands on the persons of whom they are jealous, and then are so irritable and angry, although usually gentle, that they are wont to tear their husband's hair even if he has only displeased them a few times. They are hard workers and good housekeepers, for on them depends most of the most important and most arduous work for the maintenance of their houses, the education of the children, and the payment of tribute. And with

91

all this they sometimes take on the man's work if necessary, cultivating and sowing what is needed [to feed the household]. They are wonderful husbandmen, and stay awake at night to employ the time left to them after they have attended to their homes and gone to market, in buying and selling their produce. They breed their own kinds of fowl and those from Castile to sell and to eat. They breed birds for their own recreation and for their feathers, from which they make their fine clothing. They also breed other domestic animals which they use to suckle the roe deer. In this way the latter grow so tame that they never return to the forest, although the women take them and carry them through the forest to rear them there.

They have the custom of helping each other weave cloth, and they take the same pleasure in these labors as their husbands do in working on the land, and during work they always have their mocking jokes and tell each other the news and sometimes they gossip a little. They hold it to be a great impropriety to look at the men or to laugh at them and so much so that this alone was sufficient to constitute an impropriety, and without further action to bring the woman into disrepute. They danced their dances on their own and some with the men, particularly one called *naval*, which is not very decent. They are very fertile and give birth early. They are also excellent nurses for two reasons: first, because the morning drink, which they drink hot, creates a good quantity of milk; and, secondly, because the continual grinding of maize, and the fact that they do not keep them pressed in, makes their breasts grow very large; for this reason they have a great quantity of milk.

They also became drunk at gatherings or on their own (for they eat apart), but they did not get so drunk as the men. They are a people who desire to have many children, and any woman who did not have them used to beg their idols for them with gifts and prayers, and now they ask them of God.

They are courteous and sociable to all those with whom they deal, and they are wonderfully generous. They have few secrets and are very clean in their persons and their things, for they bathe like ermines.

They were very devout and pious, and they therefore performed many acts of devotion for their idols, burning their incense before them, offering them gifts of cotton clothing, food, and drink; and it was their duty to make the offerings of food and drink that the Indians use in their celebrations. But for all this it was not their custom to spill their blood before the devils, nor did they ever do so, nor were they allowed into the temple when sacrifices were being made, except for certain feasts, when certain old women were admitted for the celebrations.

XX

During childbirth they went to sorcerers who made them believe in their lies and placed beneath their bed an idol of a demon called Ixchel, which they said was the goddess who created infants. They washed the child as soon as it was born, and once it had been freed from the agony of having its forehead and head flattened went with it to the priest so that the latter might foresee its destiny and tell it the office that it was to hold and the name that it was to bear during childhood, for they were accustomed to call their children by different names until they were baptized or grown up. Afterwards these were dropped and the children took their fathers' names until they married, and thereafter the names of both their father and mother.

These people had a great and excessive fear of death, and they showed this in that all the services which they performed for their gods served no other end, and no other purpose, than that they might be granted health and life and sustenance. When they came to die it was a sight to see how they lamented and wailed over the dead and the great sadness which death caused them. By day they wept in silence, and by night with very loud and painful cries, so that it was pitiful to hear them. They went about in deep sorrow for many days. They observed abstinences and fasts for

93

the dead, particularly for a husband or wife, and they said that the devil had taken them away, for they believe that all evils come to them from him, and, above all, death.

Once dead they shrouded the body, filling its mouth with ground maize, which is the food and drink they call *koyem*, and with it some of the stones they use as money so that in the next life he should not go without food. They were buried inside their own houses, or at the back of them, and the mourners threw into their graves some of their idols, and if he were a priest, some of his books, and if he were a sorcerer, some of his magic stones and implements. Usually they deserted the house and left it abandoned after the burial, except when there were many people living there, in whose company they lost some of the fear which the death had caused them. They burned the bodies of lords and of people of high esteem and placed the ashes in large urns and built temples over them as those which were found in Yzamal demonstrated was done formerly. Recently it was discovered that when the dead man was a very great lord they secreted his ashes in a hollow statue made of clay. The other chieftains made wooden statues for their fathers, leaving the back of the neck hollow. They then burned a part of his body and put the ashes in there and sealed it. Afterwards they stripped the skin from the back of the neck of the dead man and pasted it in place, burying the rest according to their custom. They kept the statues with great reverence among the idols. They used to cut off the heads of the old Cocom lords when they died, and after cooking them cleaned them of flesh and then sawed off half of the skull from the crown back, leaving the front part with the jawbone and teeth. They replaced the flesh that was lacking from these half-skulls with a certain bitumen and modeled them into a perfect likeness of those whose skulls they had been. And they then preserved them with the statues full of ashes. These were all kept together with their idols, in the oratories of their houses, in great reverence and respect, and during every festival and religious feast they made offerings to these statues of their food so that they should not lack for it in the next life, where they believed their souls to be resting and benefiting from their gifts.

These people have always believed in the immortality of the soul more than many other peoples—even though they may not be so civilized—for they believed that there was a more excellent life after death which the soul enjoyed on departure from the body. They said that this future life was divided into a good and a bad life, into a painful one and one full of peace. They said that the bad and the painful one was for the wicked and the good and delightful one for those who had lived well according to their beliefs. The easy life, which they said they would achieve if they were good, was to go to a very pleasant place where nothing would give them pain, and where they would have an abundance of food and drink of great sweetness and a tree which is there called *yaxche*, which is very cool and shady (and is a cotton tree), beneath whose branches and shade they would all rest and take pleasure for eternity.

The punishment for a bad life, which they said that the wrong-doers would have to suffer, was to go to a lower place than the others, which they call *Mitnal*, meaning Hell, and there to be tormented by devils and by great extremes of hunger, cold, fatigue, and misery. There was also in this place a devil and prince of all the devils whom all obeyed, and they called him in their tongue *Hunhau*.[58] They claimed that these good and evil lives had no end, because the soul had none. They also said, and held it to be absolutely true, that those who hanged themselves went to this heaven of theirs. Thus there were many who for slight reasons of sadness, troubles, or sickness hanged themselves in order to escape and to go and rest in their heaven where they said the goddess of the gallows, whom they called *Ixtab*,[59] came to take them. They had no concept of the resurrection of the body and had no record of the person from whom they had heard about this heaven and hell of theirs.

95

XXI

The sun never hides or goes far from this land of Yucatán, so the night never grows to be longer than the day; and when the nights are at their longest they are usually the same from the feast of St. Andrew to St. Lucia[60] when the days begin to lengthen. They used the Pole Star, the Pleiades, and Gemini as a guide to know the time by night. They divided the day into named parts, regulated from midday and moving east and west, by means of which names they ordered and arranged their labors. Thus their year of 365 days and six hours was as perfect as ours. They divided it into two kinds of month. One was of thirty days, which they called *U*, which means moon, which they counted from the moment it appeared until it was no longer visible. The other kind of month had twenty days. These they called *Vinal Hunekeh*, and there were eighteen of these in the whole year together with five days and six hours. From

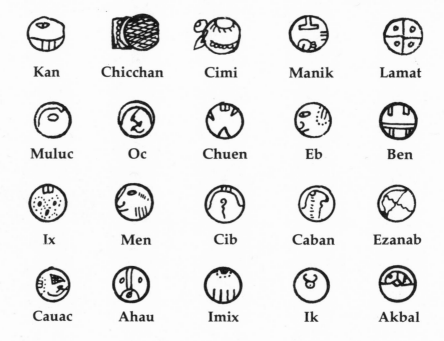

Kan   Chicchan   Cimi   Manik   Lamat

Muluc   Oc   Chuen   Eb   Ben

Ix   Men   Cib   Caban   Ezanab

Cauac   Ahau   Imix   Ik   Akbal

Landa Dæum Spectris opponit et ignibus instat.
Alphonsus pueris, iisq; prætig; docens.

Garsiaq; indigetans Crucifiæum Gentibus iussit:
Quod digitus Doctor. dextera Christ; erat.

(12)

Bischoff Landa, macht zu schanden.
Den teüffel Alphonsus wandrett.

Zur lher der haÿdn, mit den Knabn.
Garsias thuet das Creütz erhaben:

Fray Diego de Landa as Bishop of Yucatán.
From Marianus, *Gloriosus Franciscus redivivus sive chronica observantiae.*
(Copyright Bodleian Library Oxford)

Que Yucatan no es isla, ni punta q[ue] entra en la mar, como algunos pensaro[n] sino tr[ra] firme. y q[ue] se enganaron
por la punta de cotoch q[ue] haze la mar entrando la via de
la Ascension; hazia Golfo dulce. y por la punta q[ue] por esta
otra parte va a mexico hasta la desconosida antes de lle-
gar a Campeche. o por el estendimi[ento] de las lagunas q[ue] haze
la mar entrando por puerto real y dos bocas.

Que es tr[ra] muy llana y limpia de sierras, y q[ue] por esto no
se descubre desde los navios hasta muy cerca salvo entre
Campeche y Champoton donde descubren unas serrezetas
y un morro de ellas que llaman de los diablos.

Que viniendo de la vera cruz, por parte de la punta de
cotoch. esta en menos de XXi grados y por la boca de puerto real
en mas de veinte y tres y que tiene del un cabo de estos al
otro bien ciento y treinta leguas de largo camino derecho

Que su costa es baxa, y por esto los navios grandes van al
g[olf]o apartados de tierra.

Que la costa es muy suzia de peñas y pizarrales asperos
que gastan mucho los cables de los navios, y que tiene mucha
lama por lo qual aunq[ue] los navios den a la costa se pierde
poca gente.

Que es tan grande la menguante de la mar especial en
la baya de Campeche, que muchas vezes queda media legua
en seco por algunas partes.

Que con estas grandes menguantes se quedan en las ovas,
y lamas y charcos muchos pescados pequeños de que se mantie-
ne mucha gente.

Que atraviessa a Yucatan una sierra pequeña de esquina
a esquina y comiença cerca de Champoton, y procede hasta
la villa de salamanca que es el cornijal contrario al de Champoton.

Que esta sierra divide a Yucatan en dos partes, y que la
parte de medio dia hazia Lacandon, y Taiza esta despoblada
por falta de agua, q[ue] no la ay sino quando llueve. La otra
que es al norte esta poblada.

Que esta tierra es muy caliente, y el sol quema mucho
aunq[ue] no faltan aires frescos como Brisa, o solano que alli
reyna mucho, y las tardes la virazon de la mar

Que en esta tierra vive mucho la gente, y que se ha
hallado hombre de ciento y quarenta años.

Que comiença el ynvierno desde S[an]t Francisco, y dura
hasta fin de Março. porq[ue] en este tiempo corren los Nortes, y

Title page of the manuscript.

nacion, y casas por lo qual podriamos dezir se nos au
cumplido las euangelicas prophecias sobre Iherusalem de
que la cercarian sus enemigos, y ensangostarian, y
apretarian tanto que la derrocassen por tierra. Y esto
ya lo auria Dios permittido segun seriais, sino que no
puede faltar su yglesia ni lo del que dixo Nisi dñs
reliquisset semen, haut Sodoma fuissemus. —

Comiença el kalendario Romano, y Yucatanense

Ianuarius treze	dias	Meses de los Indios	
a	12	de Ben	
b	13	de Ix	
c	1	Men	
d	2	Cib	
e	3	caban	
f	4	Ezanab	
g	5	Cauac	
a	6	Abau	
b	7	Ymix	
c	8	Ik	
d	9	Akbal	
e	10	kan	Yax
f	11	chicchan	
g	12	cimij	
a	13	Mauk	
b	1	Lamat	

Van con mucho temor segun dezian
criando dioses. acabados ya, y puestos en
perfeccion los idolos hazia el dueño
dellos un presente el mejor que podia
de aues, y caças y de su moneda para
pagar con el el trabajo de los que
los auian hechos, y sacauan los de
la casilla, y poniaylos en otra rama
da para ello hecha en el patio en la
qual los bendizia el sacerdote con mucha solemnidad, y abundancia de de
uotas oraciones auiendose primero el
y los officiales quitado el tisne deque porq
dezian que ayunauan en tanto que
los hazian. Estauan untados y echa
do como solian el demonio, y quema
do el encienso. bendictos assi los poni
an en una petaquilla embueltos en
un paño, y los entregauan al dueño, y
el con asaz deuocion los recibia. lue
go predicaua el menas del sacerd...
de un poco dela excellencia del off de
hazer dioses nueuos y del peligro
q tenjan los que los hazian si a ca
so no guardauan sus abstinen-
cias y ayunos. Despues comian
muy bien y se emborachauan mejor
En qualquiera de los dos meses de
Chen, y Yax,, y en el dia que senala
ua el sacerdote hazian una fiesta
que llamauan Ocna, que quiere
dezir renouacion de templo en onra
de los chaces, que tenian por dioses
de los maizales, y en esta fiesta
mirauan los pronosticos de los
Bacabes, como mas largo queda di-
cho en los capitulos CXIII, CXIIII, CXV
CXVI, y conforme a la orden en su

A page of the manuscript.

Zaccini hecha la eleccion del principal que cele-
brasse la fiesta hazian la ymagen del demonio
llamado Zacnuayayab, y lleuauan la a los monto-
nes de piedra de la parte del norte donde el año
passado la auian echado. Hazian vna estatua al
demonio Yzamna, y ponianla en casa del principal, y todos juntos, y el camino aderecado iuan de-
uotamente por la imagen de Zacnuayayab. llegados
la sahumauan como lo solian hazer, y degollauan
la gallina y puesta la imagen en vn palo llamado
Zacbia la trayan con su deuocion y bailes los quales llaman Alcabtan Kamahau. Trayan les la beuida
acostumbrada al camino, y llegados a casa ponian
esta imagen delante la estatua de Yzamna, y alli le
offrecian todos sus offrendas, y las repartian y a la
estatua de Zacnuayayab ofrescian vna cabeça de vn
pauo, y empanadas de codornices, y otras cosas, y su
beuida. Otros se sacauan sangre y vntauan con ella
la piedra del demonio Zacacantun y tenian se assi
los idolos los dias que auia hasta el año nueuo, y
sahumauan los con sus sahumerios hasta que llegado el
dia postrero lleuauan a Yzamna al templo, y a Zac
nuayayab a la parte del poniente a echarla por ay para
recibirla otro año. Las miserias que temian este
año si eran negligentes en estos sus seruicios era
desmayos, y amortecimientos, y mal de ojos. Tenian le por ruyn año de pan, y bueno de algodon
Este año en que la letra dominical era Ix, y el
Bacab Zaccini reynaua temian por ruyn año, porq
dezian auian de tener en el miserias muchas ca
dezian auian de tener gran falta de agua, y
muchos soles los quales auian de secar los maizales
de que se les seguiria gran hambre, y de la ham
bre hurtos de hurtos esclauos, y vender a los q
los hiziessen. Desto se les auian de seguir discor

de muchas colores yno dañosas: saluo dos castas dellas
las vnas son muy ponçoñosas biuoras y mayores mucho que
las de aca de España llamanlas. taxinchan y otras ay tan-
bien muy ponçoñosas y muy grandes y con cascabel en las
colas. otras muy grandes que se tragan vn conejo y dos yno son
dañosas y es cosa de dezir que ay yndios que con facilidad
toman las vnas y las otras sin reçibir dellas perjuyzio.
Ay vna casta de lagartijas mayores que las de aca de las quales es marauilla grande el comer que los yndios tienen porque
segun ellos dizen entocandola la persª suda vn su dozillo
el qual es mortal ponçoña. Ay muchos alacranes entre las
piedras y no son tan ponçoñosos como los de aca de España.
Ay vn genero de hormigas grandes cuya picada es muy
peor y dueley encona mas que la de los alacranes, y tanto que
dura su enconaçion mas al doble que la del alacran como
he yo experimentado. Ay dos generos de arañas, la vna
pequeña y muy pestifera; la otra es muy grande y toda
cubierta de espinitas muy delicadas negras que parecen sello
y tienen enellas la ponçoña y assi se guardan mucho de
tocarlas los yndios donde las ay. otras muchas sabandi-
jas ay, pero no dañosas. Ay vn gusanito colorado del qual
se haze vnguento muy bueno amarillo para hinchazones
y llagas con no mas de batirlos, / o amasarlos juntos y sirue
de olio para pintarlos vasos y haze fuerte la pintura.

Parrapho VIII. de las auejas y su miel y cera.

Ay dos castas de auejas y ambas son muy mas pequeñas
que las nras, las mayores dellas crian en almenas las quales
son muy chicas, no hazen panal como las nras sino ciertas
bexiguitas como nuezes de cera todas juntas vnas a otras
llenas de la miel, para castrarlas no hazen mas de abrirla
colmena y rebentar con vn palito estas bexiguitas y assi corre

RELATION

DES CHOSES

DE YUCATAN

DE DIEGO DE LANDA

TEXTE ESPAGNOL ET TRADUCTION FRANÇAISE EN REGARD

COMPRENANT LES SIGNES DU CALENDRIER

ET DE L'ALPHABET HIÉROGLYPHIQUE DE LA LANGUE MAYA

ACCOMPAGNÉ DE DOCUMENTS DIVERS HISTORIQUES ET CHRONOLOGIQUES,

AVEC UNE GRAMMAIRE ET UN VOCABULAIRE ABRÉGÉS FRANÇAIS-MAYA

PRÉCÉDÉS D'UN ESSAI SUR LES SOURCES DE L'HISTOIRE PRIMITIVE
DU MEXIQUE ET DE L'AMÉRIQUE CENTRALE, ETC., D'APRÈS LES MONUMENTS ÉGYPTIENS
ET DE L'HISTOIRE PRIMITIVE DE L'ÉGYPTE D'APRÈS LES MONUMENTS AMÉRICAINS,

PAR

L'ABBÉ BRASSEUR DE BOURBOURG,

Ancien Administrateur ecclésiastique des Indiens de Rabinal (Guatémala),
Membre de la Commission scientifique du Mexique, etc.

PARIS
ARTHUS BERTRAND, ÉDITEUR
21, RUE HAUTEFEUILLE
LONDON, TRÜBNER AND CO., 60, PATERNOSTER-ROW

1864

Title page of the first printed edition of Landa's manuscript.
(Copyright Bodleian Library Oxford)

Genealogical tree of the Xiu family (1557). The figure seated
at the base of the tree is Hun Vitzil Chac Tutul. On his right
hand is his wife Yx. (Courtesy, The Peabody Museum, Harvard University)

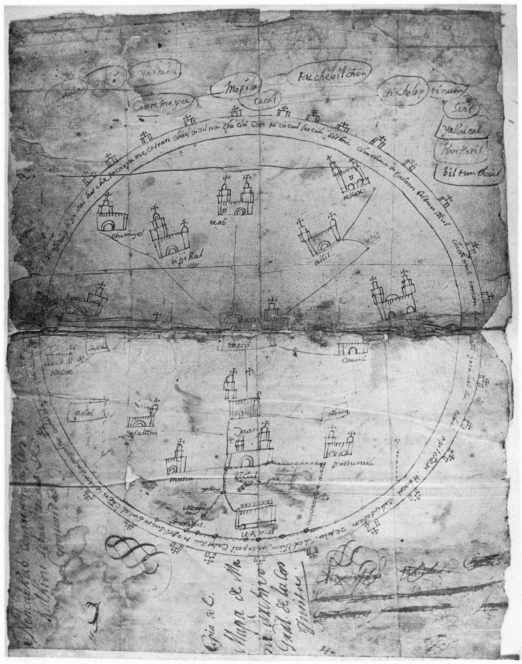

Map of the province of the Xiu. The circular form (with the capital,
Mani, at the center) is a Maya convention.(Courtesy,Latin American
Library, Howard Tilton Library, Tulane University)

Chichén-Itza: Temple of the Jaguars. (Foto INAH)

Chichén-Itza: Platform of the Eagles. (Foto INAH)

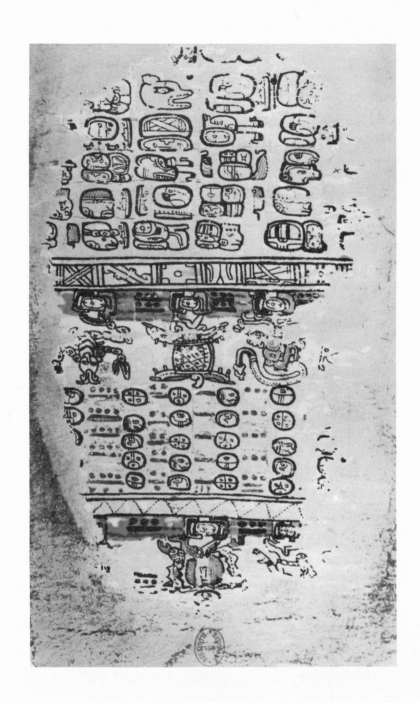

Codex Paris. (Copyright Bodleian Library Oxford)

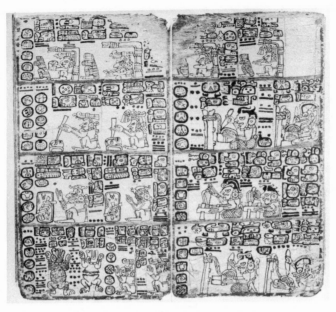

Codex Tro-Cortesianus: Troano Section.
(Copyright Bodleian Library Oxford)

Codex Tro-Cortesianus: Cortesianus Section.
(Copyright Bodleian Library Oxford)

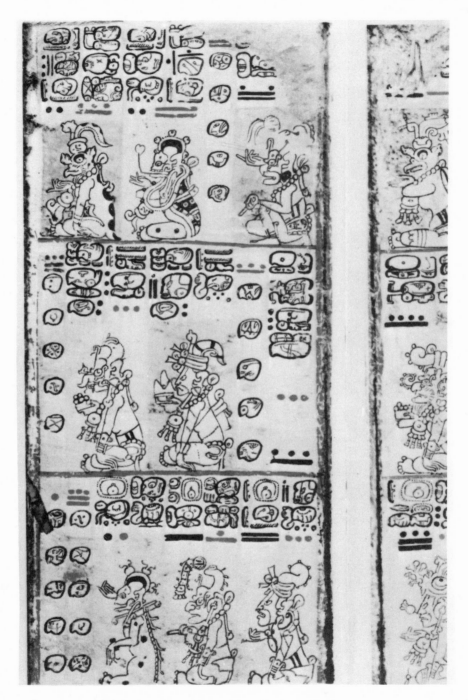

Codex Dresdan. (Copyright British Museum)

these six hours they made one day every four years and so every four years a year of 366 days. For 360 days [out of 365] they have twenty letters or glyphs with which to name them, omitting the names of the other five days, which they hold to be unlucky and evil. These letters are presented on the opposite page and beneath each one is its name so as to make it intelligible in our language.

I have already said that the Indian method of counting is by fives and from four fives they make twenty. They then take the glyph for the first digit of each of these quinary divisions and use it as we use our dominical letters to begin every first day of each month of twenty days. [This is an explanation rather than a translation. The Spanish is confused and fails to describe accurately the Maya calendar.]

| Kan | Muluc | Ix | Cauac |

Among the multitude of gods which these people worshipped were four, each one of which was called *Bacab*. These they said were four brothers whom God, when He created the world, had placed at the four corners to hold up the sky so that it should not fall. They say also that these Bacabs escaped when the world was destroyed by the Flood. They give other names to each one of these and indicate by them the part of the world where God has placed him, holding up the heavens; they also attribute to him, and to the place where he stands, one of the four dominical letters. They indicate the calamities and happy events which they said were to occur in the year by reference to these deities, every one of which is assigned a letter.

The devil, who deceived them in these matters as in others, indicated to them the rituals and offerings which they had to make to him to escape these calamities. Thus, if their prognostications

97

were not fulfilled, they said that this was because of the service they had rendered the devil; if the prognostications did come about, the priests made the people understand and believe that this was through some sin or fault in these rituals or in the people who had performed them.

The first of the dominical letters is *Kan*. The year that this letter stood for was the sign of the Bacab, whose other names are *Hobnil, Kanalbacab, Kanpauhtun* and *Kanxibchac*. This one they assign to the south. The second letter is *Muluc*, which they assign to the east, and its year was under the sign of the Bacab called *Canzienal, Chacalbacab, Chacpauahtun* and *Chacxibchac*. The third letter is *IX*. Its year was the sign of the Bacab called *Zaczini, Zacalbacab, Zacpauahtun* and *Zacxibchac* and they assigned it to the northern sphere. The fourth letter is *Cauac*. Its year was the sign of the Bacab called *Hozanek, Ekelbacab, Ecpauahtun* and *Ekxibchac*, and to this they assigned the direction of the west.

Whenever these people held a festival or solemn feast in honor of their gods they always began by driving out the devil from themselves, so as to perform it better. Driving him out was sometimes done with prayers, blessing, which they had for this purpose, and at other times with Rites, offerings, and sacrifices. To celebrate the solemn festival of the New Year these people, with much rejoicing and much dignity, according to their own unfortunate ideas, performed throughout the five days, which they held to be unlucky before the first day of their new year, many great services for the Bacabs mentioned above and to the devil whom they called by another four names, to wit: *Kanuuayayab, Chacuuayayab, Zacuuayayab* and *Ekuuayayab*, and once these rituals and festivals were ended and the devil driven out of them as we shall see, they began their new year and its festivals.

There is a custom in all the towns of Yucatán of keeping two pyramids of stones, one facing the other, at the entrance to the town, and also at the four quarters, namely east, west, north, and south, for the celebration of the two festivals of the unlucky days which they held in the following way each year.

The year whose dominical letter was *kan* was that of the deity Hobnil, and according to them both of these were assigned to the south. It was in this quarter therefore, that they made an image or hollow figure in clay of the devil called Kanuuayayab, and carried it to the pyramid of dry stones which they had raised on the southern side. They chose a prince[61] of the town in whose house the festival was celebrated on these days, and in order to celebrate it they made a statue of the devil they call *Bolonzacab*, which they placed in the house of the chieftain, in an accessible place where everyone might go. This done, the lords and the priests and the men of the town assembled and, having cleaned and prepared with arches and shady plants the road to the site of the pyramid of stone where the statue [of Kanuuayayab] was to be found, they all went along together in great devotion. Once there, the priest censed the statue with forty-nine grains of maize ground up with their incense which they tossed into the devil's brazier. They called the ground maize itself *zacah*, and that which was given to lord *chachalté*. Once the idol had been incensed, they cut off the head of a chicken and presented it as an offering. This done they set the image on a pole called *kanté*, placing on its back an angel as a sign for water and that this year was to be a good one; they painted these angels to make them look frightful. Then they carried this image, accompanied by much rejoicing and dancing, to the house of the chieftain where the other statue of Bolonzacab was standing; and from this chieftain's house they carried to the lords and priests a drink made of 415 grains of toasted maize which is called *picula kakla*, and which they all drank. When they reached the chieftain's house, they placed this image in front of the statue of the devil, which was kept there, and then made many offerings of food and drink and of meat and fish to it; later they divided these offerings among the strangers who were present. To the priest they gave the leg of a deer. Others shed their blood, by cutting their ears, and anointed with it a stone which they had there sacred to a devil called Kanalacantun. They shaped a heart out of bread and made another loaf with calabash seeds and these they offered to the image of the god *Kanuuayayab*. They attended both the statue and the idol in this way throughout the unlucky days and incensed them with an incense mixed with ground maize. They believed that if they did not perform these ceremonies they were bound to suffer certain illnesses during that year. Once these unlucky days were past they carried the statue of the devil Bolonzacab to the temple, and the idol to the eastern side of the town, so that they could go there another year and get it. There they left it and each one went to his home and busied himself with what remained to be done for the celebration of the New Year. Once the ceremonies were complete and the devil had been driven out according to their mistaken beliefs, they considered this year to be a good one for the Bacab Hobnil reigned with the letter Kan. Of him they said that he had never sinned as his brothers had done and for this no calamities would befall them during that time. But as some frequently did, the devil had arranged for the people to offer him services so that when misfortune occurred they might place the blame on the services or the servants and remain forever deceived and blind to the truth.

The devil then ordered them to make an idol, which they called Yzamnakauil, and to burn in the forecourt of the temple in his honor three balls of a kind of sap or resin called Kik and to sacrifice a dog or a man. All of these things they duly did in the way which I described in Chapter C, except that the manner of sacrifice in this feast was different. They set up in the courtyard of the temple a great pyramid of stones, and placing the dog or man whom they were to sacrifice on something higher than it, they threw the bound victim down onto the top of the stones. The priests then seized him with great celerity, took out his heart, carried it to the new idol, and offered it up between two platters. They offered other gifts of food, and at this festival the old women of the town, who had been chosen for the purpose, danced dressed in certain garments. They said that an angel descended to receive this sacrifice.

The year in which the dominical letter was *Muluc* was associated with the deity Canzienal. At that time the lords and priests elected a chieftain to perform the festival. They then made an image of the devil which they called Chacuuayayab and carried it to the pyramid of stones towards the eastern side where they had left the previous one. They made a statue of the devil called *Kinchahau* and set it in a convenient place in the house of the chieftain. And having cleaned and prepared the road they all went out from there together, observing their usual piety, to the image of the devil *Chacuuayayab*.

Once arrived, the priest incensed it with fifty grains of ground maize and their incense, which is called zacah. The priest gave the lords more incense of the kind we [*sic*] call chahalté to put into the brazier. Afterwards they cut off the head of the chicken as previously; and carrying the image on a pole called *chasté*, they bore it away while everyone accompanied it devoutly and performed some war dances called *holkanakut batelokot*. They carried out to the lords and chieftains on the road, a drink of 380 toasted maize cobs as before.

When they reached the house of the chieftain they placed the idol before the statue of Kinchahau and made all the offerings to him, which they divided up as they had done with the others. They offered the idol one loaf made with egg yolks and some others made with the hearts of deer and another with dissolved pepper. There were many who shed their blood by cutting their ears and they anointed with this blood the stone which they had there which was sacred to a devil called *Chacacantun*. Here they seized the children and drew the blood from their ears by force, slashing them with a knife. They kept their statues and idols until the unlucky days were over, during which time they burned incense before them. When the days were over they carried the image and left it on the northern side where they would go out and get it on the following year. They carried the other to the temple and afterwards went to their houses to busy themselves with the preparations for their New Year. If they did not do the aforesaid things they feared they were likely to be afflicted by the evil eye [or possibly "eye disease"].

This year, in which the letter Muluc was the dominical one and when the Bacab Canzienal reigned, they held to be a good year because they said that he was the best and greatest of these Bacab gods, for which reason they placed him first in their prayers. But for all that the Devil made them make an idol called *Yaxcocahmut*, and place it in the temple, and remove the old idols, and set up in the forecourt of the temple a block of stone on which they burned incense and a ball of resin or sap called Kik, praying there to the idol and asking him for relief from the misfortunes which they feared for that year. These were a shortage of water and an abundance of sprouts among the maize, and things of that kind, for whose prevention the Devil ordered them to offer him squirrels and an unembroidered cloth which was to be woven by the old women whose duty it was to dance in the temple for the appeasement of Yaxcocahmut. They feared many other misfortunes and bad signs, although the year was a good one, if they did not perform the services which the Devil bade them. They had to hold a festival and during it to dance a dance on very high stilts and offer the Devil the heads of turkeys and bread and maize drinks. They also had to offer him dogs made of clay with bread on their backs and the old women had to dance with them in their hands, and to sacrifice to him a little dog that had a black back and was a virgin, and the devout had to shed their blood and anoint the stone of the devil Chacacantun. They held this sacrifice and service to be pleasing to their god [Y]axcocahmut.

The year in which the dominical letter was Ix and the deity Zacini, [*sic*] they elected the chieftain who was to celebrate the feast and made an image of the devil called Zacuuayayab which they carried to the pyramid of stones on the northern side, where they had left it the year before. They made a statue of the devil *Yzamna* and placed it in the house of the chieftain, and once the road had been prepared they went piously to get the image of

Zacuuayayab. On arrival, they incensed it as they were accustomed and beheaded the chicken and placing the image upon a pole called *Zachia*, they carried it devoutly along to the accompaniment of dances called *alcabtan kamahau*. The usual drink was brought out to the celebrants on the road and when they reached the house of the chieftain they placed the image before the statue of Yzamna and there all made offerings and distributed them; and to the statue of Zacuuayayab they offered the head of a turkey and quail patties as well as other things and their kind of drink. Others drew blood and anointed the stone of the devil Zacacantun with it; and they attended the idols in this way during the days that remained before the New Year, and incensed them with their incense until the final day arrived when they carried Yzamna to the temple and Zacuuayayab to the western side and placed him there to await their return the following year.

The misfortunes they feared for this year, should they neglect these services, were faintings, swooning, and sickness of the eye. They held it to be a bad year for bread but a good one for cotton. This year in which the dominical letter was Ix and the Bacab Zaczini reigned they held to be a ruinous one because they said that many misfortunes would befall them, such as a great lack of water and a burning sun which would dry up the maize fields, from which would follow a great famine, from the famine, theft—including theft by slaves and the selling of those who did this. From this would follow discord and fights among themselves and wars with other towns. They also said that there would be changes in the government of lords and priests on account of wars and discords.

They also believed a prophecy that some of those who wished to be lords would not succeed. They said that they would be visited by locusts and that their towns would be greatly depopulated by the famine. The things which the Devil commanded them to do in order to remedy these misfortunes, all or some of which they believed would befall them, was to make an idol called *Cimchahau*

103

Yzamna and place him in the temple. There they incensed him often and made many offerings and prayers and shed their blood with which they anointed the stone of the devil Zacacantun. They held many dances, and the old women danced as they were accustomed. And at this time they built a little oratory for the devil—or renovated the old one—and in it they gathered to make sacrifices and offerings and all entered into a solemn drunk orgy, for the feast was a general one of obligation. There were some fanatics who, out of devotion and by their own volition, made another idol like the one above and placed it in other temples where they made it offerings and became drunk. These drunken orgies and sacrifices they held to be very pleasing to the idols and a measure to free them from the misfortunes of the prophecies.

The year in which the dominical letter was Cauac and the deity Hozanek, having chosen a chieftain to celebrate the feast, they made an idol of the devil called Ekuuayayab and carried it to the pyramid of stones on the western side where they had left it the previous year. They also made a statue of the devil called *Vacmitunahau* and set this up in a convenient place in the house of the chieftain. From there they all went together to the place where the idol of *Ekuuayayab* was; and they had the road well prepared for this. When they reached the idol the priest and chieftains incensed it as they were accustomed and decapitated a chicken. This done, they picked up the image on a pole called *Yaxek* and placed on the back of the image a skull and a dead man, and above it a carnivorous bird which they called *Kuch* as a sign of great mortality. They held this to be a very evil year.

They then carried it decked out in this manner, with deep feeling and devotion, and danced some dances, among which was one like the *Cazcarrientas*,[62] and so they called it *Xibalbaokot* which means "Dance of the Devil." The cupbearers appeared on the road with the drink for the lords, which they carried to the place of the statue Vacmitunahau and placed it there in front of the image which they had brought. Then they began their offerings, incensings, and prayers while many drew blood from several parts of their bodies and with it anointed the stone of the devil called *Ekelacantun*, and thus they spent these unlucky days, at the end of which they carried Vacmitunahau to the temple of Ekuuayayab in the southern sector, there to return to it the following year.

The year in which the letter was Cauac and the Bacab Hozanek reigned, they regarded as disastrous. In addition to the predicted mortality, they said that the burning sun would destroy the maize fields and that large numbers of ants and birds would consume everything they had sown. But as this would not happen everywhere, they might find food in some places with great difficulty. To remedy these misfortunes the Devil obliged them to make four devils, called *Cichacchob*, *Ekbalamchac*, *Ahcanuolcab*, and *Ahbulucbalam* and to place them in the temple where they incensed them with their censers and, as an offering, burned for them two balls of the sap or resin of a tree called Kik and certain iguanas and bread and a mitre and a bunch of flowers and one of their precious stones. In addition to this they erected in celebration of their festival, a great wooden arch, and built up the sides and the top with timber, leaving doors by which to enter and depart. After this was done, most of the men each took bundles of very long and very dry rods, and having placed a singer on top of the timber construction, this man sang and played a tune on one of their drums. All those below danced most devoutly and in an orderly fashion, going in and out through the doors of that wooden arch. They danced like this until evening when, each one setting down his bundle, they went to their homes to rest and eat.

When night fell, they returned and many people came with them, because among them this ceremony was highly regarded, and each one took up his torch and lighted it; and with these each one went for himself and set fire to the timber which blazed up and burned quickly. When it was all reduced to cinders they leveled these and spread them out wide. The dancers near there were some who, barefoot and naked as they were, began to walk across these cinders from side to side. Some crossed without harm

105

while others were scorched and some were half burned up. They believed that in this lay the remedy for their misfortunes and ill-omens, and they believed that this was the most pleasing service to their gods. This done they went out to drink and to get drunk as was required by the custom of the festival and on account of the heat of the fire.

With the letters mentioned Chapter CX the Indians gave names to the days of their months and with all these months together they composed a sort of calendar by which they arranged not only their feast days but also their numerical system, contracts, and affairs as we do with ours. They did not, however, begin their calendar on the first day of their year as we do, but long after it; and this they did because of the difficulty they had in counting the days of their months all together, as will be apparent from the calendar itself, which I here adjoin.[63] Although there are twenty letters [and days] in their months they are wont to count them from one to thirteen, and then to begin their count again from one to thirteen; and in this manner they divide the days of the year into 27 thirteens and 9 days, without counting the unlucky ones.

Despite these complications, and troublesome computations, it is a wonderful sight to see the ease with which those who are learned in it are able to count and manipulate [this calendar]. It is admirable how the dominical letter always comes out right on the first day of their year without error or exception and without any other of the twenty appearing then. They also employed this method of counting to arrive at the manner of computation which they used for the eras and other matters which, although of interest to them, is not much to our purpose and for this reason it will be enough to say that the characters of letters with which they begin their day-count or calendar is called *Hunimix* and it is thus:

It falls on no certain or fixed day because in each case the count itself is modified; nevertheless the letter, which is dominical on the first day of the following year, never fails to appear.

The first day of the year for these people was always on the sixteenth of our month of July and on the first of their month *Pop*. It is not to be wondered at that we found these people, although simple in other matters, to have a mastery and knowledge in this as other peoples have had. For according to the gloss on Ezechiel, January is the beginning of the year for the Romans; and for the Hebrews it was April; for the Greeks, March and for the Eastern peoples, October. But, although these people begin their year in July, I shall give their calendar here according to the order of our own and in conjunction with ours, so that our letters and theirs, and our months and theirs, will coincide, and will place above them their count of thirteen in order of progression.

Because there is no need to describe the calendar in one place and the feast days in another, I shall describe with each month its own feast days and the observances and ceremonies with which they were celebrated. In doing this I shall fulfill the promise I made in some previous section, namely that I would describe their calendar and at the same time describe their fasts and the ceremonies with which they made the wooden idols and other matters. In treating of these things, however, as well as the others mentioned here, my sole purpose is to provide a reason for praising God's goodness, which, having endured such things, has seen fit to remedy them in our time. So that by giving our attention to them with Christian hearts we may pray for the preservation of the Indians and for their advancement in true Christianity, and that those who are in charge of them may favor and aid them so that they may not want for help either through their own sins or ours; also so that they may not falter in what they have begun and so return to their previous misfortunes and errors, where worse things than before might befall them once the Devil has returned to the mansions of their souls from which, with laborious endeavor, we have tried to drive them out by purging these Indians and sweeping them clean of their previous vices and evil customs. And it is not unreasonable to feel fear, when we consider the perdition which has existed for so many years throughout the whole of the great and [once] most Christian Asia,[64] and in the [once] good, Catholic and Augustinian Africa, and the miseries and calamities that are happening even today in our own Europe [even] among our own people and in our own towns. In this we may say that for us the evangelical prophesies concerning Jerusalem have been fulfilled in which it was said that its enemies would encircle it and encompass it and press so hard upon it that they would tumble it to the ground. And this God would already have allowed to happen, we being as we are, but the fact that this Church cannot fail nor that which he said: *Nisi Dominus reliquisset semen sicut Sodoma fuissemus.*[65]

Here Begins the Roman and the Yucatec Calendar

January [CHEN][66]

According to their own accounts they were very much afraid of making gods. Once the idols were finished and had been perfected, their owner collected together the best gifts he could of fowl, game and some of his money, to pay the workmen who had made the idols; then they took these from their houses and placed them in another arbor, which had been built in the patio for this purpose and where the priest now blessed them with great solemnity and an abundance of devout prayers, he and the celebrants having first removed the grime. They claimed that they fasted while the idols were being made. Once they had annointed themselves, and driven away the Devil in their usual manner, and burned some of the blessed incense, they placed the idol in a small leather casket wrapped in a cloth, and then handed it over to the owner who received it very devoutly. Then that good priest preached on the excellence of the task of making new gods and on the danger run by those who performed it if by chance they did not observe all the abstinences and fasts. Afterwards they ate very well and drank still more.

YAX

In either of the months, Chen and Yax, and on the day fixed by the priest, they used to hold a feast which they called *Ocna*, which means the renovation of the temple. This feast was celebrated in honor of the Chacs whom they held to be the gods of the maize fields; and they consulted the oracles of the Bacabs in these matters, as has already been explained at greater length in Chapters CXIII, CXIV, CXV and CXVI. They celebrated this feast day every year and they also renewed the clay idols and their braziers, for it was the custom for each idol to have its own small brazier in which to burn incense for it. And if it was necessary they rebuilt or renovated the house and set on the wall a record of these things in their glyphs.

YAX

109

Imix

ZAC

Ahau

CEH

MAC

Here begins the calendar count of the Indians which in their language is called Hun Imix.

ZAC

On a day in this month of Zac designated by the priest, the hunters held another feast like the one which is held in the month of *Zip*, whose purpose was to placate the anger of the gods towards them and their plantations.[67] This they did also to atone for the blood they had spilt during the hunt, for these people abhorred the shedding of any blood unless it was in sacrifice; and for this reason they always called upon the Devil whenever they went hunting and burned incense before him. And if it was possible they also anointed his face with the blood from the heart of the game they had killed.

They held a very great feast on whatever day the seventh [day dedicated to] *Ahau* fell and this lasted for three days with incensings and offerings and their drunk pagan orgy. And, because this feast is a moveable one, the diligent priests took care to compute in advance the day on which it would fall so that they might be able to fast properly.

MAC

On any day in this month of Mac the old people held a feast in honor of the Chacs, the gods of cereals, and also of [Y]zamna. One or two days before this they performed the following ceremony, which in their language is called *Tuppkak*, they collected up every kind of field animal and insect found in their country, and gathered together in the courtyard of the temple with them. Here the Chacs and the priest sat at the corners as was their custom when casting out the Devil. Each had with him a pitcher of water which had been brought to them. In the center they placed a great bundle of dried rods, which were bound together and set upright. Then, having first burned some of their incense in the brazier, they set fire to the rods and while these were burning they tore out with

110

abandon the hearts of the birds and the animals and thew them on the fire to burn. If they could find no large animals such as tigers, lions or alligators they formed hearts out of their incense; but if they had such animals and they had killed them they brought their hearts for the fire. Once the hearts had all been consumed they put out the fire with the water from the pitchers held by the Chacs. They did all this in order to secure thereby (and also by the next feast), a year of plentiful rains for their cereals. Afterwards they celebrated the feast in a different way from the others because they did not fast for it, with the exception of the host, who did observe a fast. When the hunters arrived to celebrate the feast, the people of the town, the priest and the celebrants gathered in the courtyard of the temple where they had set up a pyramid of stones with steps, all of which was very clean and decked with branches. The priest took some incense prepared by the host which he burned in the braziers and then asserted that, at this, the Devil took flight. Afterwards they smeared, in their usual devout fashion the first step of the pyramid with mud from the well and the other steps with blue bitumen; they then burned a large quantity of incense and called upon the Chacs and upon Yzamna with prayers and acts of devotion, and made offerings of their presents. When this had been done they consoled themselves by eating and drinking the offerings with every confidence that their services and invocations would bring a good year.

MUAN

In this month of Muan those who owned cacao trees[68] held a feast in honor of the gods Ekchuah, Chac and Hobnil, who were their advocates. It was held on the property of one of their numbers where they sacrificed a dog stained the color of cacao and burned their incense before the idols offering them iguanas of the blue variety and some feathers of a particular bird, and other game. They also gave each of the celebrants a branch of the fruit of the cacao tree. When these sacrifices and prayers were over they ate

KANKIN

MAUN

111

the gifts, but, they say, that they only drank three times each from the wine for there was not enough for more. And they went to the house of the person who had taken charge of the feast and spent some time there in rejoicing.

PAX

In the month of Pax they celebrated a feast day called *Pacumchac* when all the lords and priests of both smaller and larger towns met and two together kept a vigil for five nights in the temple of *Citchaccoh* with prayers, offerings and incense, as they did during the feast of Kulkulkan, which has already been mentioned and takes place during the month of *Xul* in November. Before these days were over they all went to the house of their war captain, who was called Nacom and whom I have described in Chapter CI. They carried him with great pomp, incensing him like an idol in the temple; and they sat him down, burning incense before him. He and they then remained like this until those five days were passed, during which time they ate and drank the gifts which had been offered in the temple; they also danced a dance whose steps were like the warriors' long stride, which is why it is called *Holkanakot*, which means the "Dance of the Warriors." When the five days were over they joined the celebration which, as it concerned their wars and was to bring them victory over their enemies, was a solemn one for them. First they performed the ceremony and sacrifice of fire which I have described for the month of Mac. They then drove out the Devil with great solemnity, as was their custom, and once this had been done there came the prayers and the offerings of gifts and the burning of incense and, while the people were making these offerings and prayers, the lords took the Nacom up on their shoulders and carried him around the temple, incensing him. When they returned with him, the Chacs sacrificed a dog, by drawing his heart out, and offered it to the Devil between two dishes. Then each of the Chacs broke a large jar filled with drink; and with this they ended the feast. Once it was over they ate and drank the gifts which had been offered there, and carried the Nacom with great solemnity, but without incensing him, to his house.

There they held a great feast in which the lords, the priests and chieftains became drunk while the rest of the people returned to the towns; the Nacom, however did not get drunk. On the following day, after they had digested the wine, all the lords and priests of the town, who had been inebriated and had remained behind, gathered together in the house of the lord; and he divided among them a large amount of his incense which he had prepared and which had been blessed by those holy priests. He then delivered an oration and with much insistence commended them to observe the feasts which they were to hold in their own towns to their gods, so that the year might be rich in food. The oration over, they all departed from each other with much affection and hubbub and each one went to his town or house. There they busied themselves with their feasts which, according to how they performed them, lasted until the month of Pop. They called them *Zabacilthan* and performed them in the following manner. They sought among the richest men of the town for someone who wished to celebrate the feast and advised him of the day on which it would fall so that the three months remaining before the new year should be the more agreeable. What they did, was to gather in the house of the man who was celebrating the feast and there perform the ceremonies of casting out the Devil, of burning copal and of making offerings with dances and festivities; they also got as drunk as owls. And everything stopped for this. They went to such extremes at the feasts held during these three months that it aroused great pity to see them for some went about covered in scratches, others with broken heads or with their eyes inflamed through much drunkenness and yet despite all this they were such lovers of wine that they ruined themselves for its sake. It has already been stated in preceding chapters how the Indians began their years with the [five] nameless days during which they prepared themselves as if at

113

a vigil for the celebration of their new year. And besides the preparations made for the feast of the devil *Vuayayab*, for which they left their houses, the other preparations consisted of not going out very much during these five days and of making offerings of beads to their devils and to the other idols in the temples in addition to the gifts for the general feast. Neither the beads nor anything else offered in this way was ever employed again for their private uses. They only used some of the beads to buy incense for burning. During these days they neither combed their hair nor washed themselves; neither the men nor the women cleansed themselves of fleas, nor did they engage in any mean or heavy work for they feared that some evil might befall them if they did.

KAYAB   **CUMKU**

POP

POP

The first day of Pop is the first of the first Indian month. It was their New Year's day, and a festival much observed among them because it was a general one and for everyone when all the people together celebrated a feast day for all the idols. And so as to hold the celebrations with more solemnity on this day they renewed all the things which they used for their own domicile such as plates, bowls, stools, mats and the old clothing and shawls in which they had wrapped the idols. They swept out their [own] houses and threw on to the rubbish heap outside the town all the rubbish and old implements. No one touched these thereafter even if he had need of them. For this feast, the lords, priests and the leading persons began sometime before to fast and to abstain from their wives, along with all those others who wished to do so out of piety. They abstained for as long as they saw fit, thus some began three months before, others two, and some as they chose, but none did so less than thirteen days before. And during these thirteen days, in addition to their abstention from women, they also did not eat salt or pepper with their food. This was considered among them to be a great act of penitence. At this time they elected those officers, the Chacs, who assisted the priest who in turn prepared a large number of little balls of fresh incense as well as some small boards which the priests used and on these all the worshippers who had abstained and fasted burned the incense before the idols. Anyone who had begun his fast dared not break it for they feared that some evil would thereby fall upon their persons or upon their homes.

When the New Year came, then, all the men gathered together in the couryard of the temple by themselves, for at no sacrifice or festival performed in the temple were women allowed to be present, except for the old ones who had to dance their dances; they were allowed, however, to attend the festivals, which were held in other places. Now the men were washed clean and decked out in their red ointments and cleansed of all the black soot with which they smeared themselves when they fasted. When all had assembled with a large number of gifts of food and beverages and a large quantity of wine which they had made, the priest, who was seated in the middle of the courtyard, dressed like a pontiff, with a small brazier and the small incense platters by him, purged the temple; the Chacs sat down at the four corners and stretched a new cord from one to the other, inside of which all those who fasted were to enter so as to drive out the Devil, as I have described it in Chapter XCVI. Once the Devil had been driven out, they all began their devotions and prayers and the Chacs kindled the new fire and the priest lit the brazier which, during a feast in which everyone participated and one which was celebrated for the community [was kindled] with a new flame. They then burned incense to the Devil and the priest began to throw his own incense into the brazier. They all then came forward in turn, beginning

115

with the lords, to receive incense from the hands of the priest, which he gave to them with such solemnity and devotion that he might have been handing them relics; and this they then threw bit by bit into the brazier, waiting there until it had ceased to burn. After this incensing had finished they all ate the gifts and presents between themselves and the wine was passed around until they became rolling drunk. This was their new year, and a service very acceptable to their idols. There were some who, after this but during the month of Pop, out of piety celebrated this feast [privately] with their friends and with the lords and the priests, for the priests were always to the forefront in their celebrations and drinking.

UO

UO

In the month of Uo the priests, physicians and the sorcerers, who were all in fact the same people, began to prepare themselves for its feast with fasts and in other ways. The hunters and the fishermen came to celebrate on the seventh day of *Zip* and each of these celebrated separately on their own day. First came the day of the priests which was called *Pocam*. They gathered in the lord's house with their adornments, having first driven out the Devil according to their custom. Afterwards they took up their books and spread them out upon some green foliage which they had put there for this purpose; and with their prayers and devotions invoked an idol called *Cinchau Yzamna* who is said to have been the first priest. To him they offered their gifts and presents and burned before him over a fresh flame their little balls of incense. Meanwhile they dissolved in one of their bowls a little of [a substance resembling] verdigris with what they called "virgin water" which had been brought from a mountain where no woman had ever been; and with it they anointed the wooden end boards of their books to purify them. This done, the most learned of the priests opened a book, consulted the predictions for that year and announced them to those present; after which he preached to them for a while, charging them [to perform the necessary] safeguards against the year's evils. At this feast he also appointed the priest or lord who was to officiate the following year; and if this person were to die his children were then obliged to fulfill the dead man's duties. This done they ate all the gifts and the food which they had brought and drank until they were rolling;[69] and thus ended the feast during which they sometimes danced a dance called *Okotuil*.[70]

ZIP SEPTEMBER

ZIP

On the day following the last day [of Uo], the physicians and sorcerers together with their wives, gathered in one of their houses and the priest drove out the Devil. When this had been done they unwrapped their bundles of medicine in which they kept many childish things; each one had his own little idol to the goddess of medicine whom they called *Ix Chel* (and for this reason they called the feast *Ihcilixchel*), as well as some small stones called *Am* which they used for casting lots. In great piety, they evoked with prayers the gods of medicine who were called *Yzamna*, *Citbolontum*, and *Ahauchamahez*; and the priests gave them incense which they burned in a brazier [which they had kindled] with a new flame, while the *Chacs* smeared the idols with another blue resin like the one used in the priests' books. This done each one wrapped up the implements of his office and putting the bundles on their backs, they all danced a dance called *Chantuniab*. Once the dance was over, the men sat on one side and the women on the other and when they had cast lots for the festival of the following year, they ate the offerings and then got drunk which they did without showing any embarrassment except for the priests who are said to have been ashamed to get drunk and so kept the wine in order to be able to drink it alone at their own pleasure.

On the following day, the hunters gathered in one of their houses bringing their wives with them like the others; and the priests came and drove out the Devil as was their custom. Once this had been done they placed in the center the equipment for

117

the sacrificial offering of incense, newly kindled fire and blue pitch. And the hunters evoked by their devotions the gods of the hunt, *Acanum Zuhuyzip* , *Tabai* and others, and divided up among themselves the incense which they threw into the brazier. While it burned, each took up an arrow and the skull of a deer which the Chacs then anointed with blue pitch. And once this had been done they danced holding these in their hands. Others pierced their ears and others their tongues, passing through the perforations seven rather broad blades of grass called *ac*. Having done this first the priests and then those officiating, made offerings of the gifts; and while they danced the wine was poured out and they became too drunk to stand.

On the following day the fishermen celebrated their festival in the same manner as the hunters, except that what they anointed was their fishing tackle and they did not pierce their ears but cut them round the edges, and they danced their dance called *chocam*[71] and once this had been done they blessed a high thin pole and set it upright. After they had celebrated the festival in the villages it was the custom for the lords and many other people to go and hold it on the coast. There they fished a great deal and rejoiced greatly and took with them a great supply of nets and hooks and other implements which they used for fishing. The gods who were their patrons in this feast were *Ahkaknexoi*, *Ahpua*, and *Ahcitzamalcum*.

ZODZ

ZOTZ

In this month of Tzoz [*sic*] the owners of beehives prepared to celebrate their feast of *Tzec*; and although the chief preparation for this festival was fasting, only the priest and the officiates were obliged to fast, while for the rest it was voluntary.

TZEC

TZEC

When the day of this festival arrived the celebrants made themselves ready in the house where it was to be held; and they did everything done at the other festivals except spill their blood. They held the Bacabs, particularly Hobnil, to be their inter- mediaries. They made a large number of offerings, the most important of which were four platters that they gave to the Chacs, each of which had a ball of incense in the middle and was painted around the outside with images of honey, for the purpose for the feast was to produce an abundance of this. They concluded as usual with wine, of which there was plenty for the owners of the hives contribute large quantities.

XUL

XUL

An account was given in the tenth chapter of the departure of *Kukulcan* from Yucatán. After this even some of the Indians claimed that he had gone to heaven with the gods. For this reason they held him to be a god and fixed a time to celebrate his feast day. The entire country had observed this feast until the destruction of Mayapan. But, after the destruction, it was celebrated only in the province of Mani, while the other provinces, in recognition of what they owed to Kukulcan, presented to Mani one in one year and another the next, for, "or sometimes five," very fine feather banners which were used to celebrate this feast. This was not celebrated like those previously described but in the following manner: on the sixteenth of *Xul* all the lords and priests of Mani gathered together with a large crowd from the villages, who had already performed their fasts and abstinences when they arrived. On the afternoon of that day, they left the house of the lord where they had assembled, in a great procession accompanied by many of their actors and proceeded very quietly to the temple of Kukulcan, which had been well decked out. Once they arrived they said their prayers and set up the banners on the top of the temple, while below in the courtyard they all placed idols on the leaves of trees which they had put there for that purpose. And when the new fire had been kindled they began to burn incense in many places and to make offerings of food cooked without salt or pepper and beverages made

119

from their beans and from calabash seeds. Throughout this period they burned copal ceaselessly. The lords, and all those who had assisted, did not return to their homes for five days and nights, which time they spent in prayer and in dancing certain devout dances until the first day of *Yaxkin*. During these five days the actors went to the leading houses to perform plays and they collected up the presents they were given and carried them to the temple where, after the five days were over, the gifts were divided up among the lords, the priests, and the dancers. Then, taking up the banners and their idols, they all returned to the house of the lord whence each went his way to his own home. They said, and held it to be entirely true that, on the final day, Kukulcan descended from Heaven to receive the services, vigils and offerings. They called this feast *Chickahau*.

YAXKIN

YAXKIN

During this month of Yaxkin they began to make preparations, as was their custom, for a general feast in honor of all the gods which they also held in *Mol* on a day fixed by the priest. They called it *Olob-Zab-Kamyax* and their purpose, once they had assembled in the temple and performed all the ceremonies and burned incense as they did on previous feasts, was to anoint with the blue pitch they made, all the instruments employed in every occupation, from those used by the priest to the women's spindles and the posts which held up their houses. For this feast they gathered together all the boys and girls of the town and instead of the customary smearing and rituals they gave them nine light blows on the back of the joints of the hands. These were administered to the girls by an old woman dressed in a garment of feathers, who as she had conducted them to the ceremony was called *Ixmol* which means "the gatherer." These blows were given to them so that they might emerge as expert practitioners in the office pursued by their parents. And once the offerings had been eaten the feast ended in a drunken orgy, although one may suppose that the pious old lady took something to drink back home with her so as not to lose the feathers of her office on the way.

MOL

MOL

During this month the bee-keepers held another festival like that of *Tzec* so that the god might provide flowers for the bees.

One thing which these wretched people held to be most arduous and difficult was making idols out of wood, which they called making gods. Thus they had a particular time fixed when this was to be done. This fell in the month of Mol—or in some other month if the priest told them that was suitable. Those who wished to sponsor this task, first consulted the priest and, having heard his advice, went to the sculptors; and it is said that the sculptors always made excuses for they were afraid they they or someone in their house, would die or become fatally ill. If they accepted, however, the Chacs, whom they also elected for this purpose, began their fast. While they fasted the sponsors of the idols went in person, or sent someone, to the forests to collect the wood, which was always cedar. Once the wood had arrived they made a closed hut out of straw[72] where it was stored together with a large pitcher in which the idols were placed and kept covered while they were being made. They put out incense which they placed at the four points of the compass to burn before four devils called *Acatuns*. They laid out instruments wherewith to cut themselves and to draw blood from their ears and with these they placed the tools for carving their evil gods. After these preparations had been made the Chacs, the priests and the sculptors shut themselves in the hut and began work on the gods, during which time they frequently cut their ears and anointed with the blood those devils and also burned incense before them. They continued in this manner until the idols were complete, at which time the sculptors were given some food to eat; [and through this period] they were not allowed to consort with their wives in any way whatsoever, nor was anyone allowed near the place where they were working.

CHEN

XXII

Not only did the Indians have a year and a month count, as has been said and explained above, but they also had a way of reckoning time and their affairs by epochs. This they did using periods of twenty years, reckoning thirteen twenties by one of the twenty letters of the days of the month, which they called *Ahau*; these epochs were not in order however, but inverted as appears in the following circle:

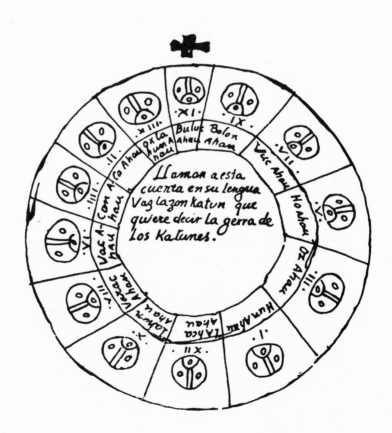

[In the middle of the diagram: "They call this count in their language *Vazlazon katun* which means the war of the *Katuns*"].

In their language these are called *Katuns* and with them they keep a wonderful record of past time and it was easy for the old man, whom I mentioned in the first chapter, to recall events that had occurred three hundred years before. If I had not known of these counts of theirs I would not have believed it were possible for them to remember things so long past.

If it was the Devil who devised this count of *Katuns*, then he did so, as he is accustomed, for his own honor; and, if it was a man, he must have been a fine idolator because with these Katuns of theirs he devised all the principal deceits, divinations and delusions under which these people labored, together with all the other misfortunes into which they had been tricked. This then was the science in which they believed most and which they valued most highly, and it was also one which not all the priests knew how to employ. The method they used when narrating their affairs and making their divinations by means of this count was to keep in the temple two idols dedicated to two of the glyphs. They worshipped, performed services and made sacrifices to the first one in accordance with the cross and the circle shown above and to secure relief from the plagues belonging to its twenty years; but in the [second] ten years that remained of the twenty from the first idol all they did was to burn incense for him and to venerate him. Once the twenty years of the first idol were over they began to follow the predictions of the second and to offer him sacrifices. They removed the first idol and replaced it by the other which they venerated for ten years. To give an example: the Indians say that the Spaniards finally reached the city of Mérida in the year of the Birth of our Lord 1541, which was the first year exactly of the era of *Buluc-Ahau* who is the one in the segment [of the diagram] marked with a cross, and that they arrived in the very month of Pop, which is the first month of the Indian year. If there had been no Spaniards they would have worshipped the idol of

123

Buluc-Ahau until the year 1551, which is ten years, and in the tenth year would have set up a fresh idol to Bolon-Ahau and paid homage to it until the year 1561, according to the predictions of Buluc-Ahau. Then they would have removed him from the temple and set up the idol Uuc-Ahau and worshipped him according to the predictions of Bolon-Ahau for another ten years; and thus they rotated all the idols. In this manner they worshipped these Katuns of theirs for twenty years, and for ten were ruled by their superstitions and deceptions, which were so many and so effective that they could deceive a simple people given to wonderment, but not those who know about the things of nature and knowledge which the Devil has of them. These people also used certain glyphs or letters in which they wrote down their ancient history and sciences in their books; and by means of these letters and figures and by certain marks contained in them, they could read about their affairs and taught others to read about them too. We found a great number of these books in Indian characters and because they contained nothing but superstition and the Devil's falsehoods we burned them all; and this they felt most bitterly and it caused them great grief. I will set down here an alphabet of these letters since their difficulty does not allow anything more. They used one character or glyph to represent all the aspirations [*aspiración*. This could mean a phoneme, a breathing or merely a sound but it is not clear whether Landa is referring to phonetics or linguistics and his descriptions make little sense in the light of modern research into Maya languages.] of their letters and then they joined on to it part of another glyph and another for joining them together, and thus these could go *ad infinitum* as may be seen from the following example: *Le* means a noose and to hunt with it. To write *Le* in their characters, we having made them understand that it is [for us] two letters, they nevertheless wrote it with three, placing as the aspiration of the *l* the vowel *e* which preceded it; in this way they make no mistakes even though they may choose to use another *e* for exactitude. For example:

e   l   e   lé

Afterwards they added the part to be joined on to the end. *Ha* means water but because *h* has *a* after it they write it both with an *a* at the beginning and at the end in the following way:

a   ha

They also write in symbols, but I did not put them down here more than was necessary except to make a complete mention of the affairs of these people. *Mainkati* means: "I do not wish" and they write it in syllables in this fashion:

ma   i   n   ka   ti

Here follows their alphabet:

A   A   A   B   B   C   T

E   H   I   CA   K   L   L

M   N   O   O   PP   CU   KU

X   X   U   P   U   Z

125

This language lacks those letters which are missing, and has added others made up from our own for other letters which they require. Now they never use these characters of theirs, particularly the young people who have learned our own alphabet.[73]

XXIII

If Yucatán had gained a name and reputation for the multitude, great size and beauty of its buildings, as other parts of the Indies have achieved with gold, silver and other riches, it would have become as famous as Peru or New Spain, for its buildings, and the great quantity that there are of them, are the most remarkable of all those things which have been discovered in the Indies to date. There are so many of them, and they are found in so many different places, and are so well built of hewn stone in their fashion that it astonishes. But as this country, although it is a good land, is not at present as [rich] as it appears to have been during the days of its prosperity, when these remarkable buildings were built in large numbers although it produces no kind of metal with which to build them. I will here give the reasons [for their construction] which I have heard given by those who have seen them. They argue that these people must have been subject to certain lords who wished to keep them occupied and they did so in this manner; and as they were such devout worshippers of their idols they distinguished themselves as a community by building temples to them. For some reason, however, they moved their towns and, wherever they settled, they always built new temples and sanctuaries and houses for the use of the lords—for they themselves have always lived in wooden houses covered with thatch. Or it may be that the great quantity of stone lime, and a certain white earth which is excellent for building, have driven them to put up so many edifices that it would sound unbelievable to all but those who have seen them for themselves. Either that, or else the country harbors some secret which, to this day has not been discovered by the natives, and has not been found out in our own time. Because it is untrue to say that these buildings were built by other nations to whom the Indians were subject; for there is evidence that they must have been built by native Indian people, as may be seen on walls and the bastions of any of the great many buildings found there, where depictions of nude men may still be seen, made modest by long girdles, which they called *ex* in their language, and by other garments which the Indians still wear today. [All these reliefs] are made of an extremely hard mortar.[74] While I was living there a large urn was discovered in a building which we pulled down. It had three large handles and was painted on the outside with silver flames. Inside were the ashes of a burned body and among these we found three good stone beads of the kind the Indian today uses for money; all of which demonstrates that the builders were Indians. It may well be that if they were, they were people of more ability than those of today and were of very much greater size and strength. This is more evident in Yzamal than in any other place for there the figures in half relief (which, as I have said are still to be seen) in mortar on the bastions, are those of large men. Furthermore, the extremities of the arms and legs of the person whose ashes were in the urn found in the building were very large and wonderfully preserved by being burned. The same may also be seen from the steps of the building which are more than two broad palms in height. But these are only to be found in Yzamal and Mérida.

Here in Yzamal there is a building standing among the others, but of such a height and beauty that it is quite astounding as will be seen from the diagram. Here is a description of it: it has twenty steps, each of which is more than two broad palms in height and width and more than a hundred feet long. These steps were made from very large hewn stones but now they are very ugly and damaged through age and exposure to water. Around it, as the circular line shows, there is a very strong wall of hewn stone from which, at a height of about one *estado* and a half, a cornice of

127

beautiful stones juts out all the way round. From these stones the building continues until it reaches the level of the square which lies at the top of the first stairway. After this square there is another staircase like the first, although not so large nor with so many steps; at the same time the wall continues all the way round the building. At the top of the steps is another fine little square on which quite close to the wall, there is a high round mound also with a staircase on its southern side—the same side where the large stairways are to be found; and on top of this staircase is a beautiful chapel of finely hewn stone. I climbed to the top of the chapel and, as Yucatán is a flat land, from there one can see as far as the eye can reach easily down to the sea itself. The buildings of Izamal were eleven or twelve in all and they all stand close together: the one mentioned above was the largest, there is no record of who the founders were but they appear to have been the first [to settle here]. The buildings stand eight leagues from the sea in a very fine site on good land and in a well-populated region, for which reason the Indians, with great insistence, made us set up a house in one of these buildings in 1549. This we call San Antonio and it has been of great assistance for spreading Christianity among them and among those round about. And so two good towns, some distance apart, have been settled on this site.

The second oldest and most important buildings in this country—and they are so old that there is no record of their builders—are those of Ti-Hoo; and these lie thirteen leagues from the ones at Yzamal and eight from the sea like those others; and there is still evidence today that there once existed a very fine highway from the one to the other. Here the Spaniards built a city and called it Mérida, on account of the great size and strangeness of the buildings, the principal one of which I will draw here as best I can as I did with that of Yzamal so as to make it easier to see what it is like.

Here is a sketch which I have been able to make of the building.

129

In order to understand it you must be clear that it is a square site of great size for it is the length of two racecourses. On the eastern side the stairway begins at ground level; it has seven steps, each the height of the ones at Yzamal. The other sides to the south, west and north are formed by a very strong thick wall. The whole of the inside of the square is paved with dry stone and at the eastern side of the quadrangle another stairway begins which, I think, is set back twenty-eight or thirty feet and is composed of more and equally large steps. The same recession occurs on the southern and northern sides but not on the west; two strong walls are then carried back until they meet the one on the western side of the square. In this way they attain the height of the stairway, all the constructions within this thus forming a solid mass of dry stones; and the height and size of this handmade mass is astonishing.

On the flat upper level the buildings begin in the following manner: on the eastern side, set within a recess some six feet deep, there is a wing, which stops short [of the walls] at both ends; and this is made of very fine hewn stone on both sides and is divided into cells, twelve feet long and eight feet wide. The doorways in the center of each of these show no signs of having had door frames or hinges but are completely smooth and made of elaborately carved stone. The work has been wonderfully executed and all the doorways are terminated on top with lintels made from a dry stone. In the middle is a passage shaped like the arch of a bridge and, above the doors to the cells, projects an apron moulding of carved stone which runs the entire length of the wing and from which some pillars extend to the roof; for half their length each of these is sunk into the wall while the other half is allowed to stand out. These small pillars rise to the height of the enclosed vaulting by which the cells are formed; on top of the little pillars another apron moulding projects around the whole block. The top has a flat roof which has been plastered and strengthened by the use of a liquid made from the bark of a tree, as is the custom. On the northern side there is another block of cells like the first except that it is only half as long. On the west there was a further block of cells, and at every fourth or fifth one there was an archway traversing the whole building like the one in the middle of the eastern block. Leading into this is a rather high, round building and then another arch leading out of it. The rest [of the block] was occupied by cells like the other. This block extends almost across the large courtyard, thus forming two patios, one at the back of it on the west and the other in front of it to the east. This latter is enclosed by four blocks, the last of which is very different from the others because it is built facing south and consists of two chambers roofed by a vault. The first of these chambers has a gallery made of very broad pillars that are closed in on top with some very beautiful hewn stones which all are made in one piece. Between the chambers runs the wall on which rests the vaults of both, with two doors by which to enter the other one. It is therefore entirely enclosed on top by plaster work.

Some stone's throw from these buildings, there is another very high-walled and beautiful courtyard in which there are three well hewn mounds of rubblework; and on top of these are some very fine chapels with vaults of the kind to which they are accustomed and skilled at making. Set well apart from this courtyard is a very large and beautiful hill and, although a large portion of the city which has been built around it has been made out of it, I do not imagine that it will ever come to an end.

The first building of the four blocks was given to us by the *adelantado* Montejo. As it had been covered by a dense thicket we cleared it and have built an adequate monastery[75] there from the stone, and also a good church which we call Madre de Dios. The old cell blocks yielded so much stone that the one on the south, and part of those to the east and west, still remain intact; so much stone was there, indeed, that we gave a great quantity of it to the Spaniards for their houses, particularly for the doors and windows.

The buildings of the town of Tikoh are not many in number nor so sumptuous as in some of the other towns, although they

131

are good and fine to look at. I would not mention them here were it not that a great population once lived in them; as it will be necessary to mention that further on I will not do so now. These buildings lie three leagues to the east of Yzamal and seven from Chicheniza.

Chicheniza is a very fine site, ten leagues from Yzamal and eleven from Valladolid, in which, according to the Indian elders, there reigned three lords who were brothers,[76] and who they remember hearing their forefathers say had come to that country from the west. And on this site they had gathered together a great company of people and settled them. They ruled the land in perfect peace and justice for several years.

They worshipped their god devoutly and therefore built many fine buildings in his honor. There was one in particular which was the largest of all and which I will now draw as I did when I was there, so that I may be better understood. They say that these lords lived without wives with great propriety and for so long as they did so they were highly esteemed and obeyed by all. Afterwards, with the passage of time, one of them disappeared and he must have died although the Indians say that he left the country from the direction of Bakhalal. His absence, however it occurred, was such a loss to those who ruled after him that they soon became corrupt in their government and so indecorous and unbridled in their behavior that the people grew to loathe them. So great was their loathing that they finally killed them and tore down and abandoned the site, leaving the buildings and the place itself, which is very beautiful because it is only ten leagues from the sea. The drawing of the main building is as follows.

This building[77] has four stairways that face the four cardinal points: they are each thirty-two feet wide with ninety-one steps so that it is tiring to climb them. The steps have the same width and height as ours. Each stairway has two low balustrades two feet wide; these are on a level with the steps and are made of finely hewn stone as is the whole building. This building has no

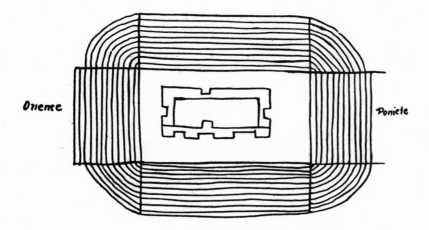

Oriente   Poniente

corners for a series of rounded stones have been built up from the ground level to the balustrades, so that the building narrows as it ascends in the most elegant way. When I saw it, each balustrade had at its foot the most ferocious mouth of a serpent, made in a single piece and very carefully carved. The stairways terminated in a small level square on the top where there was a building composed of four rooms. Three of these continue right around the building without divisions between them, and each has a door in the middle and is roofed in by a vault. The northern room is separate and in the form of a corridor resting on six pillars. The room in the interior which must have been like a small courtyard formed by the arrangement of the walls of the building, has a door that gives on to the corridor on the north side and is roofed in by wood; and it was here that they burned their incense. Above the entrance to this door, facing the corridor, is a sort of escutcheon carved in stone which I could not understand clearly.

Many other edifices once stood, and still stand today, around this one. They were all large and well built and the spaces between them were well paved. Even today there are still some remains of this paving so hard is the mortar from which it was made.

In front of the northern stairway, and set somewhat apart, were

133

two small theatres of hewn stone with four stairways paved on the top; and here they say that their plays and playlets[78] were performed for the pleasure of the public.

A fine wide causeway runs from the courtyard in front of these buildings to a well which is two stone's throw away. There was a custom, practised until recently, of sacrificing living men to the gods by throwing them into this well in times of drought; and although they never saw these men again they believed that they did not die. They also threw therein many other things such as precious stones and objects which they valued. Thus if the country had possessed any gold this well would have contained the greater part of it, so zealous were the Indians in their devotion to it. The well is seven long *estados* deep to the water and more than one hundred feet across. It is round in shape and cut out of a rock which resembles marble. The water appears to be very green but I think that this is caused by the clumps of trees which surround the well. It is also very deep. Above it, beside its mouth, there is a small building where I found images made in honor of all the principal idols of the country, almost like the Pantheon in Rome. I do not know whether this was an ancient invention or one thought out by the Indians of today so that they might encounter their idols whenever they went with offerings to the well. I found lions carved in the round and pitchers and other things, so that I do not know how anyone can say that these people did not have tools. I also found two men of great stature, each one carved out of a single piece of stone, naked but with their parts covered in the Indian fashion. The heads of their statues were made separately and had earrings in their ears as did the Indians. [The heads were fasted to the bodies by means of] a peg set into the base of the neck which then fitted into a deep hole made for it in the torso, and with this the statue was complete.

The purposes for which the Indians performed other sacrifices.

The religious feasts have been referred to earlier in the description of the calendar of these people. This shows what and how many they were, and why and how they celebrated them. But because these feasts served only to keep their gods appeased and propitious they did not go in for more bloodthirsty ones unless they considered them to be angry. They believed their gods to be angry whenever they suffered affliction from hunger, pestilence, warfare, or sterility or other such similar afflictions. Then they did not attempt to placate the devils by sacrificing animals to them or by merely making offerings of their own food and drink, or spilling their own blood, or afflicting themselves with vigils, fasts and abstinences, but forgetting all natural piety and every law of reason, they sacrificed human beings to them with as much unconcern as if they were sacrificing birds. And they did this as often as the accursed priests and the Chilans told them it was necessary or whenever the lords wished it to be done or considered it proper. As there are not so many people in this land as in Mexico and because since the destruction of Mayapan they were no longer ruled by one chief but by many, they did not carry out such a wholesale slaughter of men as in that country; but for all that many died wretchedly because each town had authority to sacrifice those whom the priest or Chilan or the lord deemed necessary. These sacrifices were performed in public places, in the temples, as though they were the most important thing in the world for the preservation of the state *(república)*. Besides the killings done in the towns, they also had those two nefarious sanctuaries at Chichenza and Cuzmil where they sent an infinite number of wretched people to be sacrified, in the one place by flinging them down the well and in the other by tearing out their hearts. May the merciful Lord, who chose to sacrifice Himself upon the cross to the Father of all, forever chose to free these men from such miseries. O my Lord God, the Light and the Being and the Life of my Soul, Holy Guide and Sure Path of my actions, Comforter in my affliction, inward joy in my sorrows, refuge and rest from my labors! What do You now command me to do Lord, what might be better called labor than rest? Whatever have You

135

obliged me to do that I am unable to accomplish most fully? Lord, do You not know the measure of my vessel and the number of my limbs and the quality of my strength? Do You perhaps, O Lord, find me wanting in my labors? Are You not the solicitous Father of the One of whom Your holy prophet has said in the psalm "I am with Him in tribulation and labor and I will free Him from it and will glorify Him?"

Lord, if You are He and the One of whom the prophet spoke when filled with Your Holy Spirit, why do You feign that to fulfill Your commands must require great hardship. For it is the case, Lord, that those who have not tasted the sweetness of the observance and fulfillment of Your precepts find hardship in them. But this is but a feigned hardship, O Lord, suffered by the fearful and the fainthearted; and those who fear it are men who never placed their hands upon the plough to accomplish it. But those who set themselves to keep Your commands find them sweet and go in pursuit of the smell of their unguents. There sweetness refreshes them at every step and each day they know more savours than they are able to describe like another Queen of Sheba. Thus, O Lord, I pray You give me grace that by Your example I may leave the house of my sensuality and the kingdom of my vices and sins and make of everything the experience of serving You and of keeping Your holy commandments, so that beyond whatever the experience of keeping them may teach me, I shall find the blessing of Your Grace for my soul by simply reading and meditating on them. Thus as I hold Your yoke to be a gentle and a light one let me give thanks to You for having protected me from its chafing and for making me free from the burdens which I see that so many multitudes of people have carried, and still carry, along the path to Hell. This is such a heavy grief that I know of no one whose heart would not break to see the fatal misery and the intolerable burden with which the Devil has always carried, and still carries, the idolators away to Hell. But if this is a great cruelty on the part of the Devil—who is the agent for it—on the part of God it is most justly permitted, because these people do not wish to rule themselves by the light of reason which He has given to them. Thus let them begin to be tormened in this life and to feel part of the hell which they deserve, for they constantly performed arduous services for the Devil accompanied by very long fasts, vigils and abstinences, incredible sufferings and gifts of their possessions and property as well as by the constant shedding of their own blood and also by the great pains and wounds which they afflict upon their bodies, and, what is worse and more serious, by offering up the lives of their neighbors and brothers. Yet for all this the Devil is never satiated nor satisfied with their torments and labors nor with carrying them off to Hell where he will torment them eternally because of these. God is appeased in a better way and is satisfied with less torments and death; for He cried out commanding the great patriarch Abraham not to stretch out his hand to take the life of his son, because His Majesty was determined to send His own Son into the world there to let Him truly lose His life upon the Cross, so that men in their misery may see that for the Son of the Eternal God the command of His Father, is a heavy one, though it is very sweet and of no account to Him. Therefore let men now give up the tepidness of their hearts and of their fear of the hardships of the Holy Law of God, for these hardships are but feigned and shortly become sweetness in their souls and their bodies, so much the more because not only is God worthy of being served and we are bound to do so by a most just duty, but all is not only for our eternal but also for our temporal benefit. Let all Christians, especially priests, consider that in this life it is a thing of great shame and disorder, and in the life to come will be more so, that the Devil should find men to serve him with such incredible efforts simply to go to Hell as a reward for them; while God can hardly find a single man who will serve Him faithfully and go to eternal glory by keeping His sweet commandments. Therefore tell me, priests of God, if you have not observed with profit the offices of these sad priests of the Devil

137

and of all those others who, we discover through the scriptures existed in past ages, and seen how much more vexations, long and numerous were their fasts than yours; how much more prolonged were their vigils and miserable prayers than yours; how much more solicitious and careful in the affairs of their calling than you in yours; and how much more zealously than you did they go about teaching their pestiferous doctrine? If seeing this you find any fault in yourself, remedy it, and consider that you are the priests of the most high God and are obliged by the calling itself to live in careful rectitude, the rectitude of an angel rather than of a man.

XXIV

I have never seen a country with so little soil as Yucatán, for the whole land is made of limestone. It really has remarkably little earth, so that there are few places where one can dig down an estado without striking great layers of limestone slabs. The stone is not very good for delicate work because it is hard and rough, but even so it was good enough for them to make out of it the many buildings that there are in this land. It is very good for producing lime, of which there is an abundance. It is a wonderful thing that this land is so fertile on and between the stone.

All that is produced there grows more abundantly where there are stones than where there is only soil so that in some places no trees will grow at all on the soil, nor do the Indians sow their seeds there and nothing grows there but grass. They sow on and among the stones and their seeds flourish there; and some of the trees grow to be so large and beautiful that they are a wonderful sight. I believe that the cause of all this is that there is more moisture, and that it lasts longer where there are stones than in the soil.

Up until today no indigenous metal has been found in this land and it is remarkable that the Indians should have built so many buildings without it and the Indians can give no information about the tools with which these buildings were built. But as they lacked metals, God provided them with a range of flint hills near that sierra which, as I said in the first chapter, runs across the land. From this they took stones to make heads for their war lances and their large sacrificial knives, of which the priests maintained a good supply, and from it they also made, and still do make, their arrowheads. In this way the flint serves them as a metal. They had a certain white brass which they mixed with a small amount of gold. From this they cast hatchets, some little bells which they used for dancing and a certain kind of small chisel with which they carved the idols and bored out their blow pipes as may be seen from the drawing in the margin.[79] They make great use of the blow pipe and shoot well with it. The people of Tabasco brought brass and other metal sheets and plates of greater hardness to trade them for devotional objects for their idols. And they had no other kind of metal.

According to the philosopher [Aristotle], one of the most necessary things for the life of man is water and so great is this necessity that without it the earth cannot give forth its fruits neither can man sustain himself. Therefore because Yucatán lacked that abundance of rivers which the neighboring countries possessed (for it only has two, one the Rio de Lagartos which flows into the sea at one extremity, and the other the Rio de Champoton, both brackish and with bad water), God provided it with many and very pretty springs and wells, some provided by nature others by dint of labor. Nature works very differently in this country as regards rivers and springs, for whereas, in the rest of the world, rivers and springs flow on top of the land, in this country they all flow beneath it through secret channels. What we discovered is that almost the entire shoreline has springs of fresh water which rise out of the sea; and it is possible to obtain water from them, as I myself have done, when the ebb tide leaves the shore almost dry. On land, God provided fissures in the rocks

139

which the Indians called *cenotes*[80] and which reach down as far as the water through the severed rock. In some of these there are such raging currents that the cattle which fall into them are at once swept away. And all these streams emerge under the sea where they form the above mentioned springs.

These cenotes contain very fine water and are a sight to see. Some are made by cutting through the rock to the water while others have several openings which were created by God, or were caused by one of the thunderbolts which often fall in these parts, or for some other cause. There are some in which a caravel would have room to sail and others that are not quite so big. Those who have access to them drew their water from them. Those who did not, dug wells and, because they lacked tools with which to do this it was very badly done. But now not only have we given them the skill to make good wells but also to make fine water wheels and tanks whence they draw their water as from a spring.

There are also lakes, all of which are filled with brackish water which is bad to drink and stagnant unlike that in the cenotes. There is one marvelous thing about the wells in this country and that is that wherever they are dug, good spring water appears, some of which is so abundant that it is a whole lance's length deep. And everywhere these are dug, a layer of conchs and small sea shells has been discovered half an estado before the water level. This is composed of as many different colors and sizes of shells as those on the seashore along with sand now turned into hard white rock. In Mani, a royal town, we dug a large well to make a water wheel for the Indians, and after having dug seven or eight estados through fine rock we came across a grave a good seven feet long full of very fresh, red earth and human bones, all of which had already almost turned to stone. There were two or three estados to go before reaching the water but before this there was a hollow vault, which God created so that the grave could be placed within the rock and it was possible to walk down it to reach the water.

We could not understand how this had come about unless we

suppose the vault had originally been accessible [from the outside] and later, because of the dampness of the cave and the passage of time, the stone had hardened and grown and so become closed in.

In addition to the two rivers which I have mentioned, this country has a spring three leagues from the sea near Campeche. It is brackish but there is none other in that entire country nor any other source of water. The Indians who live over towards the sierra have very deep wells. In the rainy season they also make cavities in the rocks to collect rainwater for their homes, because at this time long and heavy downfalls occur sometimes accompanied by much thunder and lightning. All the wells, and especially those near the sea, rise and fall every day at the times when the tide rises and ebbs, which demonstrates yet more clearly that all the water comes from the rivers which flow beneath the land to the sea.

There is a marsh in Yucatán worth mentioning, for it is more than seventy leagues long and the whole thing is a salt pan. It begins at the coast of Ekab, which lies near the Isla de las Mujeres, and continues, following the seashore between the coast and the forest until just before Campeche. It is not deep, because the lack of earth does not permit this, but it is difficult to cross going from the town to the coast or from the coast to the town on account of the trees and large quantities of mud. This marsh is so saline that God has created there some of the best salt[81] that I have seen in my life, because it is very white when crushed and those who know say that it makes such good salt that half a *celemín*[82] of it goes farther than a whole one from other places. Our Lord created salt in this marsh from rainwater, not sea water, for the sea does not enter it because between the sea and the marsh there is a strip of land running along its entire length and this separates it from the sea. In the rainy season this marsh fills up and the salt sets within the water itself, in large and small blocks that resemble nothing so much as pieces of sugar candy.

Four or five months after the rains were over, and while the

141

lagoon was still somewhat wet, the Indians used previously to go and collect salt which they did by removing those blocks from the water and taking them away to dry. They had places set aside for this purpose in the lagoon itself. These consisted of those areas most rich in salt and with the least mud and water. The Indians were not allowed, however, to collect this salt harvest without the permission[83] of the lords who had the most right in those regions on account of their proximity. All those who came to collect salt made some small donation to their lords, either of the salt itself, or of the goods produced in their lands. A chieftain called Francisco Euan, a native of the town of Cautel, established the existence of this right and he also proved that the government [*régimen*] of the city of Mayapan had settled his ancestors on the coast and given them charge of the area together with the distribution of the salt rights. The Audiencia of Guatemala therefore ordered that those who went to collect salt from his territories should now give him the same as he had previously received. A great quantity of salt is now collected at the proper time to be taken to Mexico, Honduras and Havana. Some very excellent fish breed in parts of this marsh and although they are not large they have a very good flavor.

Fish are not only found in the lagoon and the abundance on the coast is such that the Indians hardly concern themselves with the fish in the lagoon except for those who have no nets, and who kill a large number of fish in shallow water with arrows. The rest carry out their fishing on a large scale and the catch provides them with fish for themselves and for sale throughout the country.

XXV

They are accustomed to cure, grill and dry the fish in the sun without salt; and they take account of which of these methods is best suited to each kind of fish. The grilled fish keeps for several days so that they can carry it twenty or thirty leagues to sell it; and to eat it they simply cook it again and it is tasty and wholesome.

The fish which they catch and which are found on the coast are very fine and fat. There are trout and skate with exactly the same color markings and flavor as ours, but they are fattier and more tasty to eat; the Indians call them *uzcay*. There are also very good haddock and sardines and with these come sole, swordfish, mackerel, flounder and an infinite variety of other small fish. There are some very good cuttle fish on the coast of Campeche and three or four kinds of dogfish. All of these are very good and tasty; some indeed which are wonderfully tasty; and have very different heads from the others, for these are remarkably round and flat with the mouth on the inside and the eyes on the outside edge; these are called *alipechpol*. The Indians kill some very large fish which look like devil fish and they cut them into pieces and preserve them in salt. They are killed on the shore round about and are a very good thing; I do not know if this fish is a ray. There are a great number of manatees on the coast between Campeche and La Desconocida from which, besides the large amount of fish meat they produce, the Indians make quantities of lard which is excellent for cooking food. Marvelous stories are told about these manatees, especially by the author of the *Historia General de Las Indias*,[84] who recounts how an Indian lord of Hispaniola reared one in a lake and it became so tame that it came to the lake's edge when called by the name he had given it, which was "Matu." All I have to say about them is that they are so large that more meat comes off them than from a fair-sized calf, as well as a great quantity of lard. They breed like animals and for this purpose have organs like those of a man and a woman. The female always gives birth to two young, never more or less. She does not lay eggs like other fish. Manatees have two fins like strong arms with which they swim. Their head bears a close resemblance to that of an ox and they put it out of the water to eat grass on the bank. They are often attacked by bats on a round flat lip which extends all the way round the face; and they die from this because they are remarkably full of blood which gushes like water from any wound. The meat is good especially when fresh, and with mustard it is almost like good beef. The Indians kill these animals with harpoons in the following manner: they search for them in the estuaries and shallows (for it is not a fish which is able to submerge far) carrying their harpoons attached to ropes with buoys on the end. Once they have found their prey they harpoon it and release their ropes and buoys. The animal will then flee from place to place in the low and shallow water to escape from the pain caused by its wounds. But it cannot dive into the depths of the sea because these animals do not know how to. They are so large that they churn up the mud and are so full of blood that they bleed profusely; and thus the Indians follow the trail of mud in their small boats and find their catch afterwards by the buoys and then drag it ashore. It is a very agreeable fish and tasty because it is all meat and lard.

There is another fish found on this coat which they call *ba*. It is very broad and round and good to eat but it is also a very dangerous fish to kill or to encounter. Because it also is unable to swim in deep water it likes to keep to the mud, where the Indians kill it with bows and arrows. But if they are careless in approaching it, or tread on it in the water, it immediately attacks with its tail which is long and thin. This wounds so fiercely, with a saw which it carries at the tip, that it cannot be withdrawn from the place where it has lodged without increasing the size of the wound, because the teeth are reversed in the manner depicted here [drawing missing in MS]. The Indians used these small saws to cut their flesh in their sacrifices to the Devil; it was the duty of the priest to keep them and they had a large number. They are very pretty because they are of white bone and curiously fashioned into a saw so sharp and fine that it cuts like a knife.

There is a small fish so poisonous that no one who eats it escapes death in a very short time by swelling up. It often deceives people, though it is easily recognizable because it takes some time to die out of the water and swells up large itself. There are very fine oysters in the Rio de Champoton, and a great many sharks along the coast.

144

In addition to the fish whose habitat is the water, there are some kinds of creatures who live and find their food both in water and on land. Such is the iguana which is like our Spanish lizards in shape, size and color although the iguana is not so green. These creatures lay eggs in large quantities and always keep close to the sea or to places where there is water. They live both in the water and on land and for this reason the Spaniards eat them at fasting times and find them a most remarkable and wholesome food. There are so many of them that they are a great assistance to everyone during Lent. The Indians fish for them with snares which they fasten in trees and in their holes. It is remarkable how they endure hunger for it often happens that they remain alive for twenty or thirty days after capture without eating a morsel and without becoming thin. I have also heard that experience has shown that if their bellies are rubbed with sand they grow very fat. The excrement of these creatures is a wonderful medicine for curing cataracts in the eye if placed upon them when it is fresh.

There are wonderfully large turtles, some of which are much larger than a large buckler. They are good to eat and have a great deal of meat on them. They lay eggs as large as those of a chicken, laying a hundred and fifty or two hundred at a time, often making above the high water mark a large hole in the sand which they afterwards cover up again with sand; and the little turtles are hatched in these holes. There are other kinds of turtles on the land, in the dry forests and in the lakes.

Several times I saw a fish on the coast, which, as it was all shell, I left it in order to describe it here. It is the size of a small turtle, and covered on top by a round and delicate shell beautifully formed and very light green in color. It has a tail of the same substance as the shell, a span[85] long and so thin that it looks like a bodkin. Underneath it has a large number of feet all of which are filled with little eggs which are the only edible part and these are eaten a great deal by the Indians. It is called *mex* in their language.

145

XXVI

There are some very fierce alligators which, although they swim in water, come out and spend much of their time on land. They eat on land with their heads out of the water, for they lack gills and cannot chew in water. It is a heavy animal and does not stray far from the water but has a tremendous speed when attacking anything or in flight. It is a very ferocious animal and they tell strange stories about it. All I know is that one killed an Indian close to our monastery while he was bathing. A short while after this happened a religious went from the monastery with the Indians to kill it. To do this they took a dog of no great size and inserted into it, from the mouth up to the anus a very strong stick with a sharpened point; and to this they attached a very strong rope passing through the dog's intestines. When the dog was thrown into the lagoon the alligator at once appeared, seized it with its teeth and swallowed it. Once it had swallowed the dog the people who were with the friar pulled it out of the water by the rope, the stick having impaled itself in the animal's body. It was a difficult task and required much hard work. When they opened it they found in its stomach half of the man as well as the little dog. These creatures breed like animals and they lay eggs; and to do this they make large holes in the sand very close to the water and lay three hundred eggs or more, each of which is larger than a hen's egg. There they leave them until the time which nature has taught them is hatching time, when they return and wait. And the little alligators are hatched in this manner: they emerge from the eggs the length of a hand's breadth and then stay waiting for a wave to break near them. When this happens they leap from their positions into the water; but all those who have failed to reach it fall dead on the sand, for they are so tender and the sun is so hot that they get scorched and soon die. Those who reach the water all escape and at once begin to swim about in it until their parents arrive and then they follow them. In this way, although they lay a great many eggs, very few survive; and this is the work of divine providence, which has ordained that there should be more of that which is beneficial to us than that which may do us harm and could injure us, as indeed these beasts would do if they should all live.

Paragraph VII, of the kinds of serpent and other poisonous animals which there are.

There are a great variety of snakes and serpents which are many-colored and harmless except for two varieties which are very poisonous vipers and much bigger than those found here in Spain. They call these *taxinchan*. There are also others which are very poisonous and very large and carry a small rattle in their tails. There are other very large ones that can swallow a rabbit or two at one time but are not poisonous. It is remarkable that there are Indians who can catch both kinds easily without being hurt by them.

There is a breed of lizards which is larger than those here in Spain and it is remarkable how afraid of them the Indians are, for they say that whenever someone touches them they secrete a liquid which is a deadly poison. There are a great many scorpions to be found between the stones; these are not so poisonous as those here in Spain. There is a species of large ant whose sting is far worse and causes more pain and swelling than that of the scorpion; and the inflammation lasts more than twice that of the scorpion, as I myself have experienced. There are two varieties of spider, one of which is very small and venomous while the other is very large and covered all over with very delicate little black spines that resemble down and contain the poison. The Indians are therefore very careful not to touch them when there are any about. There is a small red worm from which they make a very good yellow ointment simply by beating or kneading some together and this is very good for swellings and sores. It is also used as an oil for painting bowls for it strengthens paint.

Paragraph VIII, of the bees and of their honey and wax.

There are two kinds of bee, both of which are very much smaller

147

than our own. The larger is bred in hives which are themselves very small. This bee does not make honeycombs like ours but instead a kind of small blister like a wax walnut; several of these are grouped together and are all full of honey. To collect the honey they have only to open the hive and shake these small blisters with a stick and the honey runs out. They collect the wax when they please. The others breed in the forest in the hollows of trees and stones. The Indians therefore go there to find the wax, in which this land abounds as it does in honey. The honey is very good except that it is a little watery because the food eaten by the bees is very fertile. It must therefore be boiled over a fire, but after this it is very good and long lasting. The wax is good except that it is very smoky; but the reason for this has never been ascertained. In some provinces however it is much yellower on account of the flowers. These bees do not sting nor do they do anything when the honey is gathered badly.

A remarkable variety of plants and flowers adorn Yucatán each season.[86] There are both trees and plants and many of them are wonderfully pretty and beautiful, and vary greatly both in color and smell. In addition to adorning the woods and fields, they provide a most abundant food supply for the little bees with which they make their honey and wax. I will mention some of them here as much on account of their lovely smell and beauty as for the benefit which the inhabitants of that land derive from them.

There is wormwood but it is very much more fresh and sweet smelling than the one here and it has much longer and more slender leaves. The Indians grow this plant for its smell and for their own pleasure; and I have seen that it grows more beautifully when the Indian women throw ashes around the stem.

There is a plant with very wide leaves and tall thick stems. It is remarkably strong and vigorous, so that cuttings made from the stems take so well that they grow with the same profusion as the ozier, although they are not comparable to it in any other way. When the leaf is rubbed a little it gives off a true smell of clover, although this is lost once it is dry. It is very good for decorating the temples on feast days and is used for that purpose.

There is so much basil that in some places the forest is full of it. Although it grows among the rocks it is very healthy, beautiful and fragrant; it cannot compare, however, with the basil which has been taken from here [from Spain] and cultivated in [kitchen] gardens. It is remarkable how fast it grows and spreads out covering every foot of ground.

There is a flower called *tixzula*, with the most delicate smell I have ever known, much more so than jasmine. It is white and there is also a light purple variety. As it grows from large bulbs, it could be brought to Spain. It grows in this fashion: its bulbs produce some tall, thick and very firm rush-like leaves which live the whole year through. Once a year it produces, from the middle of these, a green stem about three fingers width across and as tall and thick as the leaves themselves. The flowers grow on the end of this stalk in a cluster, each one about a span long including the stem, which produces five long open leaves. Beneath the cluster is a delicate white membrane. In the middle of the flowers there are yellow stamen. Both kinds of flower, the white and the yellow, are remarkably beautiful. When the stem is cut and placed in a jar of water it lasts giving off a delicate smell for many days because the flowers do not open all at once but only one by one.

There are some small lilies which are very white and sweet smelling and live for a long time in water. These would also be easy to transport here because they likewise are grown from bulbs. They resemble a Madonna lily in every way except that their smell is more delicate and not harmful to the head. But they do not have the yellow stamen of the Madonna lily. There is also a rose called *islaul* which they have told me is of great beauty and fragrance.

There is also a species of tree which they call *nicte* which carries large clusters of white and yellow roses with some purple ones in the middle. These are very fresh and fragrant and the Indians make very fine nosegays from them; and those who so desire also make a

149

potion from them. There is a flower they call *kom* that has such a strong smell that it burns the nostril fiercely when sniffed. It could easily be transported to Spain; and its leaves are wonderfully strong and broad. Besides these sweet-smelling flowers and plants there are others which are very useful for medicinal purposes. Among the latter are two kinds of mulberry, both of which are rigorous and very pretty to look at.

There is much ceterach and maidenhair fern and a plant whose leaves when boiled and mixed with water remove swellings from the legs and feet wonderfully well. There is another plant very remarkable for curing long-standing sores which they call *iaxpali-alche*. There is also another one which has the same taste as fennel and may be eaten; it is also very good when boiled in water for curing sores. It is applied directly like the last one. In the regions of Bacalar there is a sarsaparilla.

They have a certain plant which they grow in wells and other places. It has pointed leaves like the sedge but much thicker. From these they make their baskets which it is then their custom to dye various colors thus making them look wonderfully pretty. They have a plant which is wild but which they also grow domestically—the latter variety being the better of the two—and from this comes a kind of hemp with which they make an infinite number of things for their use. Although it is not grown domestically, they also gather a certain kind of plant that grows on trees. It produces a fruit like a small cucumber from which they make their gums and glues to stick together anything that they want to.

The crops which are available for human sustenance consist [mainly] of very good maize, in many varieties and colors. They gather it in large quantities and make granaries and store it in caverns in preparation for barren years. There are also two kinds of small bean, one black and the other multi-colored, together with another which the Spaniards have brought which is small and white. There is a native pepper and many kinds of gourds, some of which have seeds that may be used for making stews while some are eaten grilled and boiled and others are made into vessels for their use. They also have melons which are very good, and Spanish calabashes. We have set them to gathering millet which is very nutritious and grows remarkably well. They also have a wonderfully fresh and tasty fruit which they cultivate; it actually is a root which grows like a thick round turnip. This they eat raw with salt. The other kind of root, which is planted under the soil, is a great source of food and there are many different varieties, purple, yellow and white; the Indians eat them boiled and roasted and they make a very good meal. They somewhat resemble the chestnut and when roasted are used for making drinks. There are two other kinds of roots which provide sustenance for the Indians. There are also two other kinds of wild root which resemble somewhat the first two above-mentioned. They are of assistance to the Indians in time of famine, and were it not for this they would not cultivate them. There is a small tree with soft branches which holds a great quantity of milk; the leaves are eaten cooked and are like cabbages; they are very good when eaten with a large quantity of fatty bacon. The Indians plant this tree as soon as they arrive at any place where they are going to stay, and its leaves may be gathered all year round. There is also fresh chicory and although it used to grow on their plantations, they did not know how to eat it.

XXVII

And God is greatly to be praised in the words of the prophet who said, "Wonderful is Thy Name, O Lord, throughout the earth," for the great quantity of trees which the Divine Majesty has grown in the land all of which are so unlike our own that until now I have [not] seen one that I know—I mean not in Yucatán—for I have seen them elsewhere; and the Indians and even the Spaniards make use of all them for their needs.

There is a tree which has a fruit like a round gourd and from this the Indians make their vessels; these are very good, highly decorated and most attractive. There is another tree of this same species that has a smaller fruit which is very hard; from this they make some smaller vessels for ointments and other purposes. There is a tree which bears a small fruit like a hazelnut and from this they make good beads and with the rind wash their clothes as if it were soap for it lathers in the same way.

They raised a large number of incense trees for the Devil.[87] They extracted the incense from these by striking the bark of the tree with a stone so that the gum or resin flowed out from it. It is a vigorous tree, tall and with good leaves which provide shade, but where the tree is its flower blackens the bees-wax when there is any. There is a tree which they grow near their wells, and which grows beautifully high with abundant leaves. And it is remarkable how far its branches extend for they grow outwards from the trunk in neat clusters of three or more around the tree; in this way they continue to spread for as long as the main trunk continues to grow.

There are cedar trees, although not of the best. There is a kind of yellowish wood from a tree resembling the holm oak which is so remarkably hard and strong that we found it in the doorways at Izamal, used to make supporting posts which took the whole weight of the building upon them. There is another very strong wood from which they made bows and lances; and this is tawny in color. There is yet another which is dark orange in color and from which they make staves; it is very strong and called, I think *esbrasil*. There are many trees of a kind which they say are good for syphilis, and which they call *zon*. There is a tree which produces milk that is arsenical and injures anything which comes in contact with it. The shade of this tree is also most harmful especially to those who sleep under it. There is another which is covered all over with long, hard and thick thorns in pairs so that no bird can rest nor can even perch on it. There are also some hollow thorns which grow round the base of the trunk and these are always full of ants. There is yet another tree of great height and size which bears a fruit like a carob bean full of black kernels. In time of need the Indians make food of it, and from its roots they make buckets with which to draw water from the wells and for use with water wheels. There are more trees from whose bark the Indians make pails to draw water for themselves and others from which they make rope. And there are yet others from whose pounded bark they make a liquid with which to burnish the plaster work which makes it very strong. There are very beautiful mulberry trees which supply good wood and it is astounding how many other trees they have which are of service to them. In the fields and woods they have a great variety of very long osiers (although they are not really osiers) from which they make baskets of every sort and with which they bind up their houses and anything else they need to; and they are put to a remarkable number of different uses. There is a tree whose resin is a fine medicine for staining teeth red. There is another which bears a certain large fruit that provides better wool for stuffing pillows than tow from the Alcarria.[88]

Fearing that I would fail to do justice to the fruit trees and the fruit, I have decided to describe them separately, and first I shall describe their wine which the Indians value so highly that nearly all of them planted [the tree from which it was extracted] in their yards or in the open spaces around their houses. It is an ugly tree that yields only the wine extracted from its root. This is then mixed with honey and water. In the country there are some wild vines which bear edible grapes; there are many of them on the coast of Kupul. There are plum trees with many different kinds of plum; some of them are very tasty and wholesome and very different from ours for they have a little flesh and a thick rind, the reverse of those here in Spain. This tree drops its fruit before its leaves and has no blossoms only its fruit. There are many bananas, but these the Spaniards brought with them for there were none before. There is a very large tree which bears a large fruit that is quite long and wide and whose flesh is red and very good to eat. It produces no blossoms, only the fruit itself which is very small and only grows very slowly. There is another very beautiful leafy tree whose leaves never fall; and without blossoming it produces a fruit as sweet, or even sweeter, than the ones mentioned above. This is small, silky, very tasty to eat and very delicate. There are some fruits which are better than all the others, so much better indeed that they would be most highly prized if we had them in Spain. These are called in their language *ya*. There is another very beautiful, very sturdy, tree which never loses its leaves and which bears some delicious small figs called *ox*. There is another marvelously beautiful and sturdy tree which bears a fruit resembling a large egg. The Indians gather these while they are still green and ripen them in ash. Once ripe they are wonderfully sweet to eat and sugary like marzipan. There is another tree which bears another fruit, and this is also yellow but not so large as the other and softer and sweeter than it. It is remarkable in that the stone which remains after the flesh has been eaten has soft quills. There is another very shady and very beautiful tree which bears a fruit that has a shell exactly like that of a hazelnut. Inside this shell, which is a large one, it has a fruit like a morello cherry. The Indians call this *vayam* and the Spaniards *guayas*. There is a fruit which the Spaniards have brought which is good to eat and wholesome and which they call *guayabas*.

In the mountains there are two varieties of fruit trees. One bears a fruit as large as a fine pear but which is very green and has a thick skin; these they ripen by beating them against a stone, after which they have a very fine taste.[89] The other bears a very large fruit shaped like a pine cone. These are delicious to eat for they are very juicy and astringent. They have many seeds but they are not edible. There is a tree which is only found on open ground and never grows among any but those of its own species. Its bark is very good for tanning skins so it is used like a sumach. It bears a small yellow fruit which is sweet and tasty and much prized by the women. There is a very large shady tree which the Indians call *on*.[90] This bears a fruit resembling a largish gourd which is as bland as butter and it is fatty, very nutritious and sustaining. It has a large stone and a delicate skin and is eaten cut into slices like a melon and with salt.

There are some very prickly and very ugly thistles and these always grow in clumps attached to trees and winding around them. They bear a fruit which resembles the artichoke but whose skin is red, easy to peel and without thorns. The flesh inside is white and filled with small black seeds. It is wonderfully sweet and juicy so that it dissolves in the mouth; it is eaten in round slices like oranges and with salt. The Spaniards eat them faster than the Indians are able to pick them in the forests. There is a tree which, though large, is spongy and ugly; and this bears a certain kind of fruit which is full of delicious yellow fibers containing little seeds like hemp seeds but much larger. These are very good for the urine. From this fruit the Indians make a good preserve and the tree sheds its leaves after the fruit has fallen. There is a small and quite thorny tree which bears a fruit like a thin, but rather long, cucumber; it somewhat resembles the [aforementioned] thistle in taste and is eaten in the same fashion with salt and sliced. The seeds are many; small and tender like those of the cucmber. If this fruit is accidentally pierced while still on the tree a little resin with the delicate smell of civet collects in the hole. It is also good for the monthly sickness of women. There is another tree whose flower is very sweet smelling and whose fruit is the one which here in Spain is called the blancmange fruit [sic]. Of these there are many varieties all of which bear very good fruit. There is a little shrub which the Indians raise in their houses. This bears a prickly fruit which is like a chestnut although it is neither so big nor so rough. It opens when in season and inside there are some small seeds

155

which are used, even by the Spaniards, to give color to stews in the same way as saffron does; and this color is so strong that it stains deeply. I believe that there must be more fruit I ought to describe, but I have still to mention the palms, of which there are two varieties. The branches of the first are used to thatch the houses. They are very tall and thin and bear large bunches of a tasty black fruit like a chickpea to which the Indian women are very partial. The other palms are very thorny and their leaves, which are very short and thin, are of no use. They bear large bunches of a round green fruit the size of a dove's egg. Once the skin has been removed a very hard stone is left and once this has been broken open a small round kernel the size of a hazelnut is extracted. This is very tasty and useful during periods of drought, for from it they are able to make the hot food which they take in the morning; and if the need arose they could cook in its milk which is like that of almonds.

Cotton[91] grows all over the country and is gathered in extraordinarily large amounts. There are two kinds: one they sow every year; the plant is very small and lives a year. The other kind of cotton comes from a tree which lives for five or six years and bears its fruit every year. This is a nut-like pod with a green shell; it breaks open into four pieces when ripe and the cotton is found inside.

XXVIII

They used to gather cochineal[92] which was said to be the best in the Indies because the land is dry; and in a few places the Indians still gather some. There are very many varities of colorants made from the dyes of certain trees and from flowers, but because the Indians have not learned to perfect them with resins, thus giving the tones required, they have failed to produce matching colors. But the silk gatherers claim to have found a solution to this and they say that they will now be able to dye silk as well as they do in the places where the best silk is produced.

XXIX

The quantity of birds found in this land is wonderfully great; and they are so varied that He who blessedly filled it with them is greatly to be praised. They have domestic fowl such as their own kinds of hens and cocks, which they breed in large numbers in their homes, although they are difficult to raise. They have undertaken the breeding of Spanish hens and have reared such large numbers that chickens are available all year round. They breed some tame doves like ours, which multiply rapidly. They breed a certain kind of large white mallard—which I think came from Peru—for its plumage; and they frequently pluck the breasts of their birds and they want the plumage for embroidering their clothing.

There is a great variety of birds, many of which are very pretty. Among these are two species of attractive little turtle doves, both of which are very small and easy to tame. There is a small bird whose song is as sweet as the nightingale; and this they call *izyalchamil*. This lives in the walls of the houses, which have gardens, and in the trees thereof. There is a large and very pretty bird, a very dark green in color, which has only two long feathers for its tail. About halfway down and at the tip there are tufts on them. It nests in buildings and only comes out in the morning. There are other birds whose pranks and the shape of whose bodies resemble those of the magpie. They set of a loud clamour at passers-by and will not allow them to move in secret. There are many small martins or swallows; and I thought they were martins because they do not nest in the house like swallows.

There is a large and beautiful bird of many colors which has a very large and strong beak. It lives in dead trees, holding on by its talons, and strikes the trunk so fiercely with its beak that the noise may be heard from some distance away. It does this to extract from the rotten wood the worms on which it lives. These birds make so many holes that the trees in which the worms live are riddled from top to bottom.

There are many game birds all of which are good to eat. There

157

are three kinds of very pretty little doves and a bird which resembles the Spanish partridge in every particular except that its legs are very long and red in color and it feeds off carrion. It is wonderfully tame, however, if raised domestically. There is a remarkable number of quail, these are somewhat larger than ours and make a fine meal. They fly very little and the Indians catch them with dogs and nooses which they throw about their necks while they are asleep in the trees. They are very tasty game. There are many brown and colored pheasants of a reasonable size although they are not as good to eat as the ones in Italy. There is a bird as large as the European hen which they call *cambul*; it is wonderfully beautiful, very daring and good to eat. There is another called *cox*, as large as the latter and with a curious step and swagger. The males are all as black as jet and have very fine crowns of curled feathers and pretty yellow rims to their eyes. There are a large number of peacocks which, although they do not have such beautiful plumage as those here in Spain, are nevertheless very handsome and wonderfully beautiful, and as large as Indian cocks and as good to eat. There are many other birds which, although I have seen them, I cannot now remember.

The Indians kill all the large birds in the trees with arrows. They also steal the eggs from all of them and give these to their own hens to hatch so that the birds grow up very tame. There are three or four species of parrot, both small and large ones; and there are such flocks of them that they do much damage to the crops.

There are other birds which are nocturnal like the owl, the little owl and the nightjar; and it is amusing to go walking at night for they may be seen in great flocks on the road and fly along in front of one. They greatly trouble the Indians who consider them to be a [bad] omen, as they also do with other birds. There are some very carnivorous birds which the Spaniards call vultures and the Indians *kuch*; these are black with heads and necks like those of the hens here in Spain, and with a long beak like a hook. They are very dirty for they are almost always to be found in stables and in latrines eating feces and looking for dead flesh to eat. It is an established fact that until now no nest of theirs has been seen, nor is it known where they breed, for which reason some say that they live for two hundred years or more while others believe that they are the true crows. They are so good at scenting dead flesh that when the Indians wish to locate a deer which has died after escaping wounded, they climb high trees and note where these birds have gathered; and there they will certainly find their catch.

It is wonderful how many birds of prey there are and of such a large variety, for there are small eagles, some very pretty goshawks that are great hunters, and sparrowhawks which are very beautiful and larger than those found here in Spain. There are merlins and sakers and others which, as I am no hunter, I do not remember.

The infinite number, and variety, and the diversity of the sea birds, and the beauty of each species is a wonderful thing. There are birds as large as ostriches, brown and with a larger beak; they are always in the water searching for fish. When they see one they rise into the air and dive down onto it with great force and spear it with their beak, and they never miss their prey. After the attack they swallow the fish whole while swimming. There are some large thin birds that fly a lot and at a great height and the end of whose tails are split into two. The fat from these birds makes a wonderful medicine for the scars left by wounds and for shaking fits caused by wounds. There are some mallards which can stay under water for a very long time while fishing for their food. They are very agile and have hooked beaks which are small and very beautiful and these are called *maxix*. They are very tame and are reared domestically and do not seek to escape.

There are many varieties of heron and egret, some white, some brown, some large, some small. On the Laguna de Terminos there are also large numbers of these of a light red hue that resembles powdered cochineal. There are also many other kinds of birds, both small and large, and their quality and variety is a cause for

159

wonder especially when you see them anxiously searching for food on the beach. Some plunge into the water where the surf breaks and then dart away, some search for food along the shore's edge and some deprive their companions of it by reaching it first. What is even more wonderful is that God provides and showers them with blessings.

XXX

The Indians lacked many animals and above all those which man most needs to support him, but they had others which they used to maintain themselves. None of these were domesticated except for the dogs which do not bark or harm men. When out hunting, however, they could raise partridges and other birds and follow the deer over great distances since some of them were fine trackers. They are small and the Indians ate them on feast days but I believe that they are now ashamed of this and consider it a low thing to eat them. They say that they tasted very good. Tapirs are found in only one corner of this country and that is behind the mountains of Campeche. There they may be found in large numbers and the Indians told me that they are of many colors; silver grey, sorrel, bay and chestnut, while some are black and white. They are found in larger quantities in this region of the country than elsewhere for this animal is very partial to water and there are many lakes among the forests and mountains. It is as large as a medium-sized mule; it is very fleet and has a cloven hoof like that of the ox; it also has a trunk on its snout where it stores water. The Indians consider it to be a feat of great daring to kill one and the skin, or part of it, is then preserved as a relic down to the third generation; as I saw for myself. They call it *tzimin*, a name which they have also given to the horses. There are small lions and tigers which the Indians kill with bows while hiding in the trees. There is a certain kind of bear or something similar which has a great predilection for opening beehives. It is brown with a few black marks, has a round head and is long in the body but short in the legs.

There is a certain species of small wild goat which is very sure-footed and dark in color. There are hogs, which are small animals and very different to our own, for they have a navel on their backs and they stink a great deal. There is a remarkably large number of small deer whose flesh is good to eat. There is an infinite number of rabbits, all of which are like ours except that they have long muzzles which are not at all flat but resemble those of sheep; these creatures are large and very good to eat. There is a small animal which is extremely doleful by nature and moves only by night and lives in caves and hideouts. The Indians prepare a certain kind of trap for it and in this they catch it. It resembles a hare and moves nervously in bounds. It has very long narrow front teeth; its tail is smaller even than that of the hare and it is of a yellowish color. It is wonderfully tame and friendly and is called *zub*.

There is another small animal which looks like a suckling pig, and has the forefeet and the snout of a great burrower. It is covered all over with delicate scales so that it resembles an armoured horse with only its ears, feet and forefeet showing and with its neck and forehead covered in scales. It is very good and tender to eat.

There are other animals like small dogs; these have heads like pigs and long tails, are smoky colored and so remarkably sluggish that they may often be caught by the tail. They are very greedy and wander about the houses at night and kill off all the chickens one by one. The female gives birth to fourteen or eighteen off-spring at a time. These resemble small weasels, have no hair and are remarkably slow-moving; for which reason God has provided the mother with a strange pouch in the belly where she shelters her small ones. A piece of skin grows along the entire width of the abdomen from one side to the other [below] the teats. When she seals this up the teats are shut off; and when she wishes to she opens it and each of the young ones is given a teat to suck. When she has them all attached to her in this way she closes up

161

the flap of skin, presses it tight so that none can fall out and thus burdened goes off in search of food. They are reared like this until they have hair and are able to walk.

There are foxes just like those here in Spain, except that they are not so big nor do they have such fine tails. There is an animal called a *chu* which is remarkably mischievous, as large as a small dog, and with a snout like a suckling pig. The Indian women breed them and there is nothing which they do not root up or overturn. They are remarkably fond of playing with the Indian women who delouse them; and the dogs follow the women about everywhere, and never in their lives will they have anything to do with men. There are many of these and they always travel in herds in a line, one behind the other, with their snouts placed beneath the tail of the one in front. They do much harm in the maize fields which they happen to cross. There is a small animal like a white squirrel with some dark yellow bands around it which is called a *pay*. This protects itself by urinating against all who harm it. The stench which its discharges gives off is so horrible that no one can endure it nor can anything which happens to fall into it ever be used again. They have told me that it is not urine but a kind of fluid which this animal carries in a little sac in its rear. Whatever it may be, it is most effective in its defense and rarely do the Indians kill it. There are some very pretty little squirrels and moles and weasels and many mice like the ones in Spain except that they have very long snouts.

XXXI

The Indians have not lost by the arrival of the Spaniards but have gained a great deal even in small affairs, although these are very important. They have been given a great number of things from which, as time goes on, they must needs come to benefit, indeed they have already begun to benefit from and to utilize many of them. There are already a large number of good horses and many mules of both sexes. Donkeys do badly however and I think that this is because they have been too well treated, for the donkey is a sturdy animal and kind treatment only harms it. There are many very fine cows, large numbers of pigs, sheep, ewes, goats and some of our own European dogs which give good service and must therefore be counted among the useful things. There are cats which are very useful and necessary in those parts; and the Indians are very fond of them. Also among the useful things are chickens and pigeons, oranges, limes, citrons, grapevines, pomegranates, figs, guava and date trees, bananas and melons and other fruits and vegetables. Only melons and gourds are raised from their own seed, while fresh seed for all the rest have to be brought from Mexico. Silk is now grown there and it is very good.

They now have tools and have learned how to handle them very well and have been taught mechanical skills. They now also use money and many other Spanish things, which, although they managed without them before and could manage without them now, they live incomparably more like men and with them and by them are assisted in their manual labors which are thereby made the more easy, for according to the words of the Philosopher: Art aids nature.

Not only has God, by the arrival of our Spanish people, blessed the Indians with the abovementioned things, which are so essential for the livelihood of man (and these cannot be paid for merely with the tasks which the Indians have performed—or may yet perform for the Spaniards) but they have also received without charge those things which can neither be bought nor earned, namely justice and Christianity and the peace in which they now live. These they owe principally to Spain and to her people and in particular to her most Catholic kings (who, by means of continuous care and great Christianity, have always preserved them in [justice and Christianity]) to whom they are more greatly indebted than to their first founders, wicked fathers who reared them in sin and as children of wrath, whereas Christianity rears them in grace

163

in order to enjoy Eternal Life. Their first founders did not know how to govern them so that they might be protected from the many kinds of error in which they lived. Justice, by means of preaching, has led the Indians from their erroneous ways and will not prevent them from returning to them; but if they do return they must be drawn out again by means of reason. Rightly then may Spain glory in God for He chose her from among all other nations to save so many people; for this reason then, the Indians owe to her much more than they do to either their founders or ancestors for, as the blessed Saint Gregory says, to be born would be of little benefit to us if we were not redeemed by Christ, our Saviour. Likewise, we may ask like Anselm, what benefit we gain by being redeemed if we do not obtain the fruit of our redemption, which is salvation? Therefore, those who claim that, because the Indians have been injured and tormented and set bad examples by the Spaniards, they would have been much better off if they had never been discovered, are gravely in error, for they suffered far greater injuries and torments from their own people by constantly killing, enslaving and sacrificing each other to the Devil. If the Indians have been given bad examples, or continue to be given them by some, the king has rectified this and continues to do so each day with his laws *(Justicias)* and through the constant preaching and persistent opposition of the friars to all who set, or have set, bad examples to the Indians. But it is an evangelical doctrine that bad examples and scandals are necessary and I believe this to have been the cause among these people in order that they might learn, by separating the gold from the dross and the grain from the chaff, how to value virtue, as indeed they have done understanding with the Philosopher[93] how virtue shines among vices and the virtuous man among the sinful. He who has set them a bad example or exposed them to scandal must suffer his own terrible castigation unless he does penance by means of some good deed. And you, dear Reader, also ask God on your own behalf, and receive my slender work, overlooking its defects and remembering, whenever you come upon them, that I do not defend them. Saint Augustine says that Cicero claimed never to have written any work he wished to recall and this did not please the saint for it is in man's nature to err. But at the beginning [of my work] and even before you come upon my mistakes you will find that I have acknowledged and revoked them in my introduction and prologue. You may judge, as did the blessed Augustine in his epistle to Marcella, the differences between the man who confesses his errors or mistakes and the one who defends them, and must therefore forgive me mine, because the prophet says that God will forgive both of us: Lord I said I would confess my wickedness and injustice and at once you pardoned me.

XXXII

The historian of the affairs of the Indies [Oviedo], to whom much is owed in those lands for the light which he has shed upon them says, in speaking of Yucatán, that the Indians used to fight, with slings and sticks whose points had been hardened by burning. I have already mentioned in Chapter CI the weapons which they used in war and I am not surprised that when Francisco Hernández de Córdoba and Juan de Grijalva were routed in Champoton they belived that the stones which the Indians threw at them had been launched from slings. But they do not, in fact, know how to use a sling nor have they ever seen one although they can throw a stone very hard and with accuracy by aiming at their target with the left arm and index finger. He also says that the Indians are circumcised, and the reason for this may be found in Chapter LXXXXIX. He also says that there are hares but you will find a description of what this animal in fact looks like in paragraph XV of the previous chapter. He says that these are partridges and you will find a description of these in paragraph XIII of the previous chapter. Our historian further adds that crosses are said to have been found on Cape Catoch among the dead and the idols. He does not believe this however because no crosses could have been erected by the Spaniards who left Spain after it was lost,[94] for they would have had to touch first on some other land for there are many of these. I myself do not disbelieve it for this reason, which, does not convince me because we know less about any of these other places where they might have landed or which they might have reached before they came to Yucatán (if indeed they did come), as we do about the country of Yucatán itself. The reason why I do not believe it, however, is that when Hernández and Grijalva landed at Catoch their intention was not to dig up the dead but to look for gold among the living. I also believe in the power of the Cross and in the wickedness of the Devil who would not suffer a cross among the idols for fear that one days its strength would shatter them miraculously and they would all fly against him and confound him as the ark of the Scripture did to Dagon, although this was not consecrated with the blood of the Son of God nor sanctified by His divine limbs as is the Holy Cross. But in spite of all this, I will set down what I was told by an Indian lord who was a man of good understanding and high reputation among the Indians. One day, when we were discussing this subject I asked him if he had ever received any news of Christ our Lord, or of his Holy Cross. He replied that he had never heard anything from his ancestors about Christ or about His Cross but once, while tearing down a small building in a certain part of the coast, they had found in some graves metal crosses upon the bodies and bones of the corpses. They had not thought about the cross again until now when they were Christians and saw it worshipped and adored; from this they suppose that those dead men also must have been Christian. If this was so, it is possible that a few people from Spain reached Yucatán and because they died out shortly afterwards no record of them has survived.

Here ends the manuscript of the account of the affairs of Yucatán.

Notes

1. This account is not to be found in the manuscript.

2. Salamanca de Chetumal. Seven of the Spanish settlements established in Yucatán between 1527 and 1544 bear this name. A list with the dates of their foundation and names of their founders is given in Tozzer, p. 257.

3. This statement is incorrect; a number of settlements are known to have existed on the shores and islands of Lake Petén. One was visited by Cortés on his journey to Honduras. Roys (quoted in Tozzer, p. 4, n. 10) suggests that Landa is referring to the dry country to the north of the lake.

4. For an account of this expedition, see Wagner, *The Discovery of Yucatán by Francisco Hernández de Córdoba*, which provides annotated translation of all relevant material.

5. An army commander with administrative and judicial authority over the lands he conquered.

6. Juan de Grijalva came from the same Spanish town (Cuéllar, province of Segovia) as Diego Velázquez and was rumored to be his nephew. An account of his voyage by Juan Diaz, the chaplain of the fleet, may be found (in an English translation) in Fuentes, *The Conquistadors*, pp. 5-16.

7. Christopher Columbus's son Diego who, on his father's death, succeeded to the title of Grand Admiral of the Ocean Sea. At this time he was also governor of Hispaniola, having replaced Nicolás de Ovando in 1509.

8. This word is of Arawak origin. It meant "chief of a tribe" on the island of Hispaniola and was first brought to Central America by the Spaniards. During the colonial period it came to be applied there only to the headmen of *cabeceras*, or provincial capitals, who were entrusted with the task of tribute collection. On this term and its linguistic history, see Ricardo E. Alegría, "Origin and Diffusion of the Term 'Cacique.'" On the role of the cacique in colonial Mexico, see Charles Gibon, *The Aztecs under Spanish Rule*, pp. 194-267 *passim*.

9. Cortés left Santiago de Cuba on November 18, 1518.

10. Anton de Alaminos was Columbus's pilot on the latter's final voyage in 1502. He sailed with Hernández de Córdoba, Grijalva and Cortés to Yucatán and with Ponce de León to Florida.

11. Literally, "the bay of the bad fight."

12. "Friends let us follow the cross and if we have faith by this sign we shall conquer"—a free version of the device employed on the imperial standard of Constantine the Great (A.D. 306-387).

13. The word *hidalgo* is derived from Old Spanish *fijo de algo*. It originally meant a person of the noblest descent but, by the sixteenth century, the term had come to be used of the lower and often landless nobility.

14. A round ship of some hundred tons, burden, or more. Like all such classifications at this time, the term does not imply any specific rig, although a *nao* was always square-rigged.

15. For a dicussion of the role of Marina in the conquest of Mexico and of her relationship with Cortés and Aguilar, see Pagden, *Hernán Cortés*, pp. 464-465.

16. Marina spoke Nahuatl as her mother tongue. This she translated into Chontal Maya for Aguilar, who then translated that into Spanish. Later she may have acquired some knowledge of Spanish herself, since she accompanied Cortés to Honduras as an interpreter without Aguilar.

17. The word *principal* has been translated as "chieftain," for it is unlikely that Landa intended it to carry any more precise meaning. During the colonial period, however, the term was generally only employed of an official in command of a *barrio*, or district, of an Indian town.

18. This is Yucatec Maya, which was spoken by most of the inhabitants of the Yucatán Peninsula from the fifteenth until the mid-seventeenth century. Although it had a number of regional dialects, it was a remarkably uniform language compared with those of the central Mexican area. For a classification of the various languages of the Maya group, see McQuown, "The Classification of Mayan Languages."

19. The fullest account of Chichen-Itza may be found in Tozzer, "Chichen Itza and its Cenote of Sacrifice."

20. Tozzer, p. 19, n. 118, reads *sus* (their). A dotted *i*, however, is clearly visible in the MS., giving *sin*, "without."

21. A vertical unit of measurement used for depth and height and roughly equivalent to the average height of a man.

22. This is the Mexican deity Quetzalcoatl, whose name is interpreted variously as "Precious-Twin" and "Plumed Serpent." Originally a Toltec tribal chieftain (?), he had come, by the time of the Spanish Conquest, to occupy a significant, if somewhat ambiguous, position in the Mexican pantheon. In the account of Quetzalcoatl's history given by Bernardino de Sahagún (*Florentine Codex*, vol. 3, pp. 31-35) he is depicted as a messianic figure deceived by the machinations of sorcerers and forced to leave his natural home; before leaving, however, he promises one day to return and reclaim his own. It is impossible to ascertain how far this legend has been modified by contact with Christian beliefs and by its role in the donation of Montezuma and subsequent attempts to justify the Spanish conquest of Mexico. (See Pagden, *Hernán Cortés*, pp. 467-469, for a brief survey of this problem.) Landa's account resembles that of Sahagún in its broad outline and, although this might at first suggest an identity between the two Quetzalcoatl cults, it is to be remembered that Landa was a member of the same order as Sahagún, Andrés de Olmos and Toribio de Motolinía, all of whom wrote extensively about the subject. Furthermore, Landa offers no further description of the cult or of the way in which it was celebrated, and we may assume that the Maya absorbed it into what was an already flourishing native religion.

   Quetzalcoatl was also regarded by the Spaniards as having been responsible for the introduction of idolatry into Yucatán (Tozzer, pp. 22-23, quotes from some of the sources for this belief) and for having taught the Maya to practice human sacrifice.

23. For a description of the site of Mayapan see Gordon R. Willey and William R. Bullard, Jr., "Prehistoric Settlement Patterns in the Maya Lowlands," pp. 368-370.

24. A system of forced labor originally introduced to evade the laws against slavery. For a discussion of the term and its uses, see F. A. Kirkpatrick, "*Repartimiento-Encomienda*."

25. According to Cogolludo (*Historia de Yucatán*, quoted by Tozzer, p. 28, n. 155), these books were called *analta*, but this sounds like a corruption of the Nahuatl word *amatl*, the name of the bark paper of which the "books" were made. Bernal Díaz (chap. 27) says that they were called *amales*, a word which has been modified by contact with Spanish. *Analteh* and *anares* are other variants found in the works of the colonial writers. The Yucatec word was *huun*. Only three Mayan "books," now misleadingly called codices, have survived: these are: the Codex Dresden, the Codex Madrid or Tro-Cortes and

169

the Codex Paris (see plates 12-15), all of which deal with the passage of time, calendrical computations and, perhaps, religious rituals. Their full meaning has yet to be revealed. (For a description of these manuscripts see Thompson, *Maya Hieroglyphic Writing*, pp. 23-26, and, on their manufacture, Von Hagen, *The Aztec and Maya Papermakers*.)

26. Born Nachi Cocom, he was *Halach Uinic*, or territorial ruler, of the Indian state of Sotuta. The dates of his birth and death are unknown, but he was already Halach Uinic in 1536, when he murdered the Xiu ruler who was on his way to the *cenote* at Chichen-Itza (see p. 55) and was still alive at the time of the Mani law treaty of 1557. His reputation for learning is attested to by Serapio Zumarraga of Mani, who claimed that he was a great magician and had once made a man pregnant. (Roys, *The Titles of Ebtun*, pp. 6-7.)

27. An *alcalde*, in the sense in which the term is used here, was an officer who served on a *concejo* or municipal council, and exercised a measure of judicial power. Montejo was not, however, an *alcalde del rey*, since Cortés, and not the king, was responsible for his appointment. (For an explanation of the events leading up to the founding of Veracruz, see J. H. Elliott's introduction to Pagden, *Hernán Cortés*, pp. XI-XXXVII.)

28. Adrian of Utrecht was regent of Castile from 1520-1522. In 1522 he was created Pope Adrian VI.

29. For a succinct account of the conquest of Yucatán by Montejo, see Scholes and Roys, *The Maya Chontal Indians*, pp. 123-141.

30. *Que el adelantado Montejo no pobló a propósito de quien tiene enemigos:* Tozzer (p. 52), and other editors, postulate an omission by the copyist following *a propósito*. The sentence, however, makes perfect, albeit rather clumsy, sense as it stands.

31. The holder of a *licenciatura*, the second of the Spanish academic degrees, which carried with it certain valuable privileges, among which was the right to be tried in an ecclesiastical court for most offenses.

32. The *audiencia* was a royal court of justice with defined territorial jurisdiction. In the Indies the *audiencia* shared in the government of the colony where it had been established.

   The Audiencia de los Confines was first established at Gracias a Dios, in Honduras, in 1543. Alonso Maldonado was its first president and Alonso López de Cerrato its second. In 1549 it was transferred to Guatemala City and renamed the Audiencia de Guatemala.

33. Most Mayan cities have been considered to be essentially temple enclosures rather than urban settlements. This idea, however, has frequently been challenged, and in the light of recent research it now seems certain that some cities at least supported quite large urban populations. Mayapan, for instance, is believed to have supported some eleven thousand to twelve thousand

inhabitants during the Late Post-Classic period. The pattern of concentric zoning described by Landa—although it is known to have existed at Mayapan —does not appear to have been general (Pollock, Roys, Proskouriakoff and Smith, *Mayapan, Yucatán, Mexico*, part 3.)

34. A routine local judicial inquiry into the way a crown official had carried out his duties. It was usually held at the end of a term of office, and the holder was not allowed to leave his post without having submitted to it first.

35. The Royal Council of the Indies, created in 1524 and consisting of a president and eight councilors, was entrusted with handling on the crown's behalf all administrative, judicial, and ecclesiastical matters relating to the Indies.

36. He allotted to each settler his *repartimiento* (assignment, see n. 24) of Indians.

37. Jacques "de Testera" was a Frenchman and a brother to the chamberlain of Francis I. He first went to America in 1529, and there became custodian of the Franciscan order in New Span. In 1535 he went to Yucatán and was among the first religious to remain for any length of time in that peninsula. His name is associated with "Testerian hieroglyphs"—a form of picture-writing devised to teach the catechism to the Indians (see Tozzer, p. 67, n. 303).

38. Toribio de Benavente, who adopted the Nahuatl sobriquet *Motolinía* ("the poor one") on his arrival in Mexico, was one of the original twelve Franciscans who reached New Spain in 1524. Motolinía was one of the earliest chroniclers of Indian life, but only two of his works have survivied: the *Historia de los indios de la Nueva España* and the *Memoriales*.

39. Luis de Villalpando became in 1549 the first custodian of the Franciscan order in Yucatán. He was the first Mayan scholar of note and is said to have been the author not only of the grammar here mentioned but also of a dictionary. Brinton (*The Maya Chronicles*, pp. 74-75) claims that this later work was published in Mexico City in 1571. Icazbalceta (*Bibliografía Mexicana*, p. 41) lists other references to the work but was unable to see a copy. The signs and pebbles were used as mnemonic aids. For a description of Villalpando's method, see Tozzer p. 69, n. 312.

40. Antonio de Mendoza, third son of Iñigo López de Mendoza, count of Tendilla, marquis of Mondéjar, the first viceroy of Granada, was himself the first viceroy of New Spain and succeeded Cortés in the government of the colony. He was appointed in 1535 and ruled for fifteen years.

41. A holder of Indians under the *encomienda* system. Landa employs the term as synonymous with *repartimiento* (see n. 24).

42. A judge or magistrate of an *audiencia* (see n. 32) or chancellery.

43. He was appointed *oidor* of the Audiencia de los Confines in 1548 and came to Yucatán as visitor in 1552. His ordinances, promulgated between 1552 and

1553, attempted to introduce many of the reforms of the New Laws of 1542. They are printed by Ancona, *Historia de Yucatán*, vol. II, pp. 538-558.

44. *Sacerdotes:* despite the use of a term which he employs constantly of the native Indian priests, Landa is probably referring here to the Spanish secular clergy with whom the Franciscans came frequently into conflict.

45. This method of seeking to convert the mass of the people through educating or indoctrinating the sons of their leaders was a common practice. Martin de Valencia, superior of the first Franciscan mission to New Spain, adumbrated just such a policy in a report to the king made as early as 1532 (*Colección de Juan Bautista Muñoz*, vol. 61, f. 120r).

46. A yellow penitential garment used by the Inquisition which a reconciled heretic wore hanging from his shoulders.

47. Toral was the first resident bishop of Yucatán. An able scholar who could speak Nahuatl and had written a grammar and vocabulary of the Popoloca language of Puebla, it was he who ordered Bernardino de Sahagún to write his famous history (see n. 22). For his dealings with Landa see Introduction, pp. 13-17.

48. This statement may be a copyist's misreading. The Yucatán Maya are, in fact, fairly short and thick-bodied; the average height for men is 5'1" and for women 4'8". (Morley, *The Ancient Maya*, p. 23. See also Steggerda, *Maya Indians of Yucatán*.)

50. Culhua, the name given to the lands of the Mexica Confederacy, the so-called "Aztec Empire." On the geography of this area, see Barlow, *The Extent of the Empire of the Culhua-Mexica*.

51. The principal articles of exchange were cacao, which was used throughout Mexico, beads made of red shells, jade, and green stones resembling jade, small bells and copper hatchets (see n. 56), (Tozzer, pp. 95-6, nn. 417-418.)

52. The principal areas of trade of the Yucatec Maya were Nicaragua, the Guatemalan highlands, some areas of Chiapas, the lands of the Mexica Confederacy and probably some parts of Oaxaca. The items exchanged, as Landa suggests, were largely luxury goods and the raw materials for their manufacture. The economy of the tribe as a whole remained a strictly domestic one. Because of the enormous distances to be covered, traders set up ports of exchange on the bay of Chetumal, at Xicalanco, and at the head of the gulf of Honduras, the latter to serve as an outlet for the cacao-producing area centered round the town of Nito. (See Anne M. Chapman, "Port of Trade Enclaves in Aztec and Maya Civilizations.")

53. *Coroza:* the pointed paper cap placed on a criminal's head as a sign of infamy and specially, at an *auto de fe*, on the heads of heretics handed over to the secular power for execution.

54. Gonzalo Fernández de Oviedo y Valdés. The first part of his *Historia general y natural de las Indias* was published at Seville in 1535; book XX of the second part appeared at Valladolid in 1557. The rest of the work remained unpublished during the author's lifetime. Landa appears to have had access to both printed works, on which he draws heavily. The note on circumcision occurs in lib. XVII, cap. XVII (p. 533) of the 1851 Madrid edition of the complete work.

55. This passage appears, written by the same hand, in the margin of the MS.

56. Probably a copper alloy with a small admixture of gold. These hatchets were important items of trade (see n. 51) and according to Peter Martyr (*De orbe novo*, dec. III, cap. 4) were among the goods carried in the canoe discovered by Columbus among the Bay Islands on his fourth voyage.

57. The Spanish text reads, *aperrear*: the Spaniards frequently punished Indians by setting their dogs on them.

58. Hun Ahau or I Ahau appears as a calendrical name for Venus at heliacal rising. I Ahau, however, is more often associated with terrestrial darkness as an aspect of creation and bears little relation to the Christian devil. The whole passage indeed suggests an oversimplified Christian interpretation of Maya eschatalogy (see Thompson, *Maya History and Religion*, pp. 300-304).

59. Ix Tab ("she of the cord"). This figure probably, in fact, represents the moon goddess. She appears depicted with a rope around her neck in the eclipse tables of the Codex Dresden (see Thompson, "The Moon Goddess in Middle America").

60. St. Andrew's Day falls on 30 November in the Julian calendar and that of St. Lucia on 13 December (10 and 23 December respectively by the Gregorian count). The feast of St. Lucia marks the beginning of the winter solstice and has the longest night of the year.

61. The manuscript here reads *príncipe*. If the copyist's reading is correct, it is doubtful whether Landa intended by it to convey the sense of any office or function other than those generally associated with lords *(señores)* or chieftains *(principales)*. It is possibly a scribal error for *principal*.

62. *Cazcarrientas*: Tozzer (p. 147) translates the term as "muddy dance," presumably deriving an etymology from *cazcarria*, "filth" or "mud." Since a "muddy dance" is an unlikely prospect, it is possible that the name retained the meaning of the Latin root given by Corominas (*Diccionario crítico etimológico*, vol. I, p. 738), *cascus*, "old." The *cazcarrientas* would therefore mean "the dance of the old men," which would seem to fit the context. I have been unable to discover any other reference to a Spanish dance of this name.

63. Mayan calendrics are highly complex and, as yet, only imperfectly known. For a general discussion of the problem, see Linton Satterthwaite, "Calendrics

173

of the Maya Lowlands." Numerous hypothetical correlations with the Christian calendar have been suggested. The most generally accepted are those of Spinden *(The reduction of Maya Dates)* and Thompson ("Maya Chronology: the Correlation Question" and *Maya Hieroglyphic Writing),* although these differ by some 260 years. A recent attempt was also made by C. H. Smiley to produce a correlation based on astronomical data ("The Antiquity and Precision of Maya Astronomy") but this has not yet acquired wide recognition.

64. "Asia" was, at this time, a loose geographical term often extended to include the Middle East. The author of such an influential treatise as the *Semeiança del Mundo* (c. 1223), for example, held that *Asia interior* reached from the Indus to the "West." By Christian Asia, Landa probably means the Christian kingdom of Jerusalem rather than the Byzantine Empire.

65. Issaiah I:9. The text of the Vulgate in fact reads: *Nisi dominus exercitum reliquisset nobis semen quasi sodoma fuissemus et quasi Gomorra similes essemus."* The King James Bible gives the verse as, "Except that the Lord of hosts had left unto us a very small remnant, we should have been as Sodom, we should have been like unto Gomorrah." Landa, no doubt quoting from memory, completely distorts the sense of the passage.

66. In Tozzer, *op. cit.,* this calendar has been recorded so as to correspond to the Maya, rather than Christian, calendars. The day signs have also been omitted. Landa's computations are based on the Julian calendar, to which ten days must be added to bring it into line with the Gregorian calendar.

67. *Contra ellos y sus sementeras:* the sense of this passage seems to be that the purpose of the festival was to prevent disfavor falling upon the entire tribe for the action of the hunters. It is likely, however, that the act of breaking the soil when planting was regarded in much the same light as the act of killing when hunting, and that the expiatory rites were also shared by the planters.

68. *Cacahuates:* this word is only used once by Landa. It is derived from the same Nahuatl root as Spanish *cacao–cacahuatl* or *cacuatl*—which refers to the cocoa bean rather than to the plant (Siméon, *Dictionnaire de la langue nahuatl,* p. 47).

69. *Hacerse zaques:* a common expression at this time for extreme drunkenness. Covarrubias *(Tesoro de la lengua castellana,* p. 394) claims a Toledan origin for it. Tozzer (p. 154) translates literally, "until they were sacks of wine."

70. *Okotbil:* Kurath and Martí *(Dances of Anáhuac,* p. 32) suggest that this term is the equivalent of the Mexica *Netecuitotilo,* the "lordly dance," which was performed every four years.

71. *Chohom:* "dance of the fishermen." This was a fertility ritual performed round a large tree trunk set upright on the shore. It may be identical with the ribbon or maypole dance described by Clavigero *(Historia antigua de México,* p. 269).

72. *Ritual of the Bacabs*, p. 12, where a "straw house" *(dzulbal)* is mentioned. Such houses were also named for trees, e.g., in the *Book of Chilam Balam* (pp. 63-64), and associated with lineage cults.

73. This "alphabet" is, so far as many be ascertained, a series of glyphs for the objects or actions which in Maya most closely approximated the sounds of the Spanish letter. Thus when Landa asked his informant to write down the letter *b*, which in Spanish is pronounced like English *bay*, he drew a foot, the symbol for travel, *be* in Maya meaning a journey. The implications of this, of course, reflect little credit upon Landa's ethnographical methods. The alphabet, however, is not so useless as has sometimes been supposed, and Thompson has even described it as being "as close to a Rosetta stone as we are ever likely to get" (*Maya Hieroglyphic Writing*, p. 28). The problems of decipherment of the Maya glyphs are too complex to be considered here. The best work on the subject is Thompson's compendious *Maya Hieroglyphic Writing* and a recent short pamphlet, *Maya Hieroglyphs without Tears*. Thompson has also catalogued most identifiable glyphs in *A Catalog of Maya Hieroglyphs*.

74. Maya mortar and the plastar used for mural and stucco was produced by mixing quicklime with calcareous sand *(sascab)* and water (Robert C. West, "Surface Configuration and Associated Geology of Middle America," p. 73).

75. This building was described by Stephens in 1843, who noted that the outer of the two parallel corridors was supported by a Maya vault (*Incidents of Travel in Yucatán*, vol. I, pp. 92-94. See also Tozzer, p. 177, n. 925).

76. During the famous Valladolid lawsuit of 1618, two witnesses, when questioned about the Itza migration, provided different versions to the one here given by Landa. According to one, a group came from Mexico—by which he presumably meant nothing more specific than the lands beyond Yucatán and Campeche— some of whom established themselves at Chichen-Itza, others at Bacalar (Bakhalal) while others settled in the coastal regions in the north. The leader who settled in Chichen-Itza was called Cupul. According to the second witness, the invaders were led by four members of a single family; one settled at Chichen-Itza, one at Bakhalal, one on the north coast and one on Cozumel (Brinton, *The Maya Chronicles*, pp. 114-118, Thompson, *Maya History and Religion*, p. 12). In the light of these statements it would seem possible that Landa's account was modified by contact with prevailing ideas about Mexican migratory myths (see n. 22).

77. This building is the one now known as the Castillo.

78. *Farsas y comedias*. Tozzer (p. 179) translates as "farces and comedies," but neither word necessarily implies that the performances were comic ones.

79. This drawing is missing from the MS.

80. From the Yucatec Maya *tz'onot*, meaning a well. The *cenote* is, in fact, a sink formed by the caving of surface rock above subterranean channels. In addition

175

to the *cenotes*, Yucatán also has a large number of shallow water depressions known as *aquadas*. These geological features have dictated, to a large extent, the location of Maya settlements. Roys prints maps of the relationships between settlements and water deposits in the southern Cupul area in *The Titles of Ebtun*, plates 1, 2. See also Pearse, *et al.*, *The Cenotes of Yucatán*.

81. Salt was an important article of trade upon which most of the commercial prosperity of northern Yucatán depended. The quantities which could be drawn from the salt beds far exceeded anything which was produced by the saline springs of southern Mexico or the deposits of the Laguna de Terminos (De Mendizabal, "Influencia de la sal en la distribución geográfica de los grupos indígenas de México").

82. *Celemín*, a dry measure. When used of grain it was equivalent to the twelfth part of a *fanega*, which was itself the equivalent of 1.58 bushels.

83. Disputes over these salt rights frequently gave rise to outbreaks of warfare, accounts on which may be found in the *Relaciones de Yucatán* (vol. 2, pp. 86, 90). Under Spanish rule they were granted to local *caciques* (see n. 8).

84. See n. 54.

85. *Jeme*: the distance between the thumb and index finger when fully outstretched (Corominas, *Diccionario crítico etimológico*, vol. 2, p. 1046). This is not a true equivalent of the English span, which is the distance from the thumb to the tip of the little finger.

86. For the correct nomenclature of all the flora described by Landa see Tozzer, pp. 194-201, nn. 1030-1100.

87. The copal tree.

88. The Alcarria region to the northeast of Madrid was one of the chief grazing areas of Castile. Landa's birthplace, Cifuentes, is in this region.

89. Probably a prickly pear.

90. The avocado pear.

91. Cotton in the form of wraps *(mantas)* was an important item of trade before the Conquest.

92. *Grana*, more properly kermes—the dye made from cochineal.

93. The philosopher mentioned here and on page 139 is Aristotle. Landa appears to be alluding to Books II-V of the *Nichomachean Ethics*, but the vagueness of the reference suggests that he knew this work only at second hand, perhaps through the gloss of St. Thomas Aquinas. He may, however, have had access to the translation made by Charles, Prince of Viana, from the Latin Version of Leonardo Bruni, which was published in Saragossa in 1509. This translation included Aquinas' gloss.

94. I.e., during the Arab invasions of A.D. 711-716.

176

Bibliography

Manuscript Source

Real Academia de la Historia, Madrid, Colección de Juan Bautista Muñoz. MS. Signatura A. 106.

Books

Alegría, Ricardo E., "Origin and Diffusion of the Term 'cacique,' in the Acculturation of the Americas," *Proceedings and Selected Papers of the XXIX International Congress of Americanists,* edited by Sol Tax (Chicago, 1952), pp. 313-315.

Ancona, Eligio, *Historia de Yucatán desde la época más remota hasta nuestros días*, 4 vols (Barcelona, 1889).

Aristotle, *La philosofia moral del Aristotel: es a saber Ethicas: Polithicas: y Economicas: en Romance* [trans. by Carlos, príncipe de Viana] (Caragoça, 1509).

Barlow, Robert H., *The Extent of the Empire of the Culhua-Mexica* (Berkeley and Los Angeles, 1949).

Brinton, D. G., *The Maya Chronicles* (Philadelphia, 1882).

Chapman, Anne M., "Port of Trade Enclaves in Aztec and Maya Civilizations," *Trade and Market in the Early Empires*, edited by Karl Polanyi *et al.* (Glencoe, Illinois, 1957), pp. 114-153.

Chi, Gaspar Antonio, *Relación*. In Tozzer, *Landa's Relación de las cosas de Yucatán*, pp. 230-232.

Chilam Balam. The book of Chilam Balam of Chumayel [translated and edited], by Ralph L. Roys (Norman, 1967).

Clavigero, Francisco Saverio, *Historia antigua de Mexico*, 4 vols (Mexico, 1945).

Codex Dresden: Die Maya-Handschrift der Königlichen Bibliothek zu Dresden, herausgegeben von Prof. Dr. E. Förstemann (Leipzig, 1880).

Codex Tro-Cortesianus, [Codex Madrid] *Museo de América, Madrid*. Introduction in German and English summary by F. Anders (Graz, 1967).

Codex Peresianus [Codex Paris] *Bibliothèque Nationale, Paris*. Introduction in German and English summary by F. Anders (Graz, 1968).

Cogolludo, *see* López de Cogolludo, Diego.

Corominas, J., *Diccionario crítico etimológico de la lengua castellana*, 4 vols (Bern, 1954).

Cortés, Hernán, *Hernán Cortés: Letters from Mexico*, translated and edited by A. R. Pagden (New York, 1971).

Covarrubias, Sebastián de, *Tesoro de la lengua castellana o española*, (Madrid, 1611; revised edition: Madrid, 1674), ed. Martín de Riquer (Barcelona, 1943).

Díaz de Castillo, Bernal, *Historia verdadera de la conquista de la Nueva España*, edited by Joaquín Ramírez Cabañas, 6a. ed., 2 vols (Mexico, 1960).

Documentos para la historia de Yucatán, edited by F. V. Scholes, C. R. Menéndez, J. I. Rubio Mañé and E. B. Adams, 3 vols. (Mérida [Yucatán], 1936-1938).

Fernández de Oviedo y Valdes, Gonzalo, *La historia general*. [Colophon: Fin de la primera parte de la general y natural historia de las Indias y tierra firme de mar océano . . .] (Seville, 1535).

————— , Libro XX. *De la segunda parte de la general historia de las Indias . . .* (Valladolid, 1557).

————— , *Historia general y natural de las Indias islas y tierra firme del mar océano,* edited by José Amador de los Rios (Madrid, 1851).

Fuentes, Patricia de, *The Conquistadors* (New York, 1963).

García Icazbalceta, Joaquín, *Bibliografía mexicana de siglo XVI: Catálogo razonado de libros impresos en México de 1539-1600,* new edition edited by Agustín Millares Carlo (Mexico, 1954).

Gates, William, *see* Landa, Diego de.

Genet, Jean, *see* Landa, Diego de.

Gibson, Charles, *The Aztecs under Spanish Rule* (Stanford and London, 1964).

Herrera, Antonio de, *Historia general de los hechos de los castellanos en las islas y tierra firme de mar océano,* 4 vols (Madrid, 1661).

Icazbalceta, *see* García Icazbalceta.

Kirkpatrick, F. A., "Repartimiento-Encomienda," *The Hispanic American Historical Review,* XIX (1939), pp. 372-379.

Kurath, Gertrude Prokosch and Samuel Martí, *Dances of Anahuac, The Choreography and Music of preCortesian Dances.* Viking Fund: Publications in Anthropology, 38 (New York, 1964).

Landa, Diego de, *Relation des choses de Yucatán de Diego de Landa: Texte espagnole et traduction française en regard.* Collection de documents dans les langues indigènes pour servir à l'étude de l'histoire et de la philologie de l'Amérique ancienne, 3 (Paris, 1864).

————— , *Relation des choses de Yucatán: Relación de las cosas de Yucatán. Texte espagnol et traduction française en regard,* edited by Jean Genet, 2 vols [incomplete] (Paris, 1928-1929).

————— , *Landa's "Relación de las cosas de Yucatán." A Translation.* Edited with Notes by Alfred M. Tozzer, Papers of the Peabody Museum of American Archaeology and Ethnology, Harvard University, XVIII (Cambridge, Massachusetts, 1941).

————— , *Yucatán before and after the Conquest by Friar Diego de Landa with Other Related Documents, Maps and Illustrations.* Translated with notes by William Gates. Maya Society Publication, 20 (Baltimore, 1937).

—— , *Manuscrito de Diego de Landa tomada directamente del único ejemplar que se conoce y se conserva en la Academia de la Historia.* [Transcribed by Juan de Dios de La Rada y Delgado] (Madrid, 1879).

—— , *Relación de las cosas de Yucatán.* Introducción por Angel María Garibay K. (Mexico, 1966).

—— , *Relación de las cosas de Yucatán por el P. Diego de Landa, obispo de esa diócesis. Con un apéndice en el cual se publican por primera vez varios documentos importantes y cartas del author.* Introducción y notes [by Hector Pérez Martínez]. (Mexico, 1938.)

[*Doctrina christiana traducida en la lengua de los indios de Yucatán por Fray Diego de Landa.* Title supplied by Medina *op. cit.*, I, p. 378. No copy of this work has come to light but Landa mentions it in a letter of 1578 as, "printed in this city [Mexico] while I was there." (H. Pérez Martínez, *op. cit.*—see previous entry—documento 4.)]

Lizana, Bernardo de, *Historia de Yucatán, devocionario de Nuestra Señora de Izmal, y conquista espiritual* (Valladolid, 1633).

López de Cogolludo, Diego, *Historia de la provincia de Yucathan* (Madrid, 1688).

[López Medel, Tomás] *Tratado cuyo título es De los tres elementos, aire, agua i tierra en que se trata de las cosas en cada uno dellos, acerca de los ocidentales Indias . . .* In Real Academia de la Historia, *Colección de Juan Bautista Muñoz*, vol. 27, pp. 125-128.

Marianus, *Gloriosus Franciscus redivivus sive chronica observantiae* (Ingolstadt, 1625).

Martyr, Peter (Anglerius), *De orbe novo* (Alcalá, 1530).

De Orbe Novo. The Eight Decades of Peter Martyr D'Anghera. Edited and translated by F. A. MacNutt, 2 vols (New York, 1912).

McQuown, N. A., "The Classification of Mayan Languages," *International Journal of American Linguistics,* XXII (1956), pp. 191-195.

Medina, José Toribio, *La imprenta en México (1539-1821)*, 4 vols (Santiago de Chile, 1907-1912).

Mendizabal, Miguel de, "Influencia de la sal en la distribución geográfica de los grupos indígenas de México" In *Proceedings of the XXIII International Congress of Americanists,* (New York, 1930) pp. 93-100.

Momigliano, A. P., "The Place of Herodotus in the History of Historiography." In *Studies in Historiography*, (London, 1969) pp. 127-142.

Morley, Sylvanus G., *The Ancient Maya*. Third edition revised by George W. Brainerd (Stanford, 1956).

Motolinía, Toribio de Benavente, *Motolinía's History of the Indians of New Spain*. Translated and edited by F. B. Steck, Academy of American Franciscan History, Documentary Series, No. 1 (Washington, 1951).

——— , *Memoriales o libro de las cosas de la Nueva Espagna y de los naturales de ella*, new edition edited by Edmundo O'Gorman (Mexico, 1971).

Pagden, A. R., *see* Cortés, Hernán.

Pearse, A. S., *et. al.*, *The Cenotes of Yucatán*, Carnegie Institution of Washington, Publication No. 457 (Washington 1936).

Pollock, H. E. D., R. L. Roys, T. Proskouriakoff and A. L. Smith, *Mayapan, Yucatán, Mexico*, Carnegie Institution of Washington, Publication No. 619 (Washington, 1962).

Oviedo, *see* Fernández de Oviedo y Valdés.

Roys, R. L., *The Titles of Ebtun*, Carnegie Institution of Washington, Publication No. 505 (Washington, 1939).

Relaciones de Yucatán, vols. 11 and 13 in *Colección de documentos inéditos relativos al descubrimiento, conquista y organización de las antiguas posesiones españolas de ultramar*. Second series (Madrid, 1898-1900).

Ritual of the Bacabs: A Book of Maya Incantations, translated and edited by Ralph L. Roys (Norman, 1965).

Sahagún, Bernardino de, *Florentine Codex: General History of the Things of New Spain*. Trans. [from the Nahuatl] by Arthur J. O. Anderson and Charles E. Dibble, 12 vols (Santa Fe, New Mexico, 1950-1963).

Satterwaite, Linton, "Calendrics of the Maya Lowlands." In *Handbook of Middle American Indians*, (Austin, 1965) vol. 3, Pt. 2, pp. 603-631.

Scholes F. V., and E. B. Adams, *Don Diego Quijada, alcalde mayor de Yucatán*, 1561-65, 2 vols (Mexico, 1938).

——— and R. L. Roys, *Fray Diego de Landa and the Problem of Idolatry in Yucatán*, reprinted from Carnegie Institution of Washington, Publication No. 501, pp. 585-620 (Washington, 1938).

181

————— , and R. L. Roys, *The Maya Chontal Indians of Acalan-Tixchel*, second edition (Norman, 1968).

Siméon, Rémi, *Dictionnaire de la langue nahuatl ou mexicaine* (Graz, 1963).

Semeiança del Mundo, edited by W. E. Bull and H. F. William (Berkeley, 1959).

Smiley, C. H., "The Antiquity and Precision of Maya Astronomy," *Journal of the Royal Astronomical Society of Canada*, LIV (1960), pp. 222-226.

Spinden, J. H., "The Reduction of Maya Dates," *Papers of the Peabody Museum*, Harvard University, VI, No. 4 (1924).

Steggerda, Morris, *Maya Indians of Yucatán*, Carnegie Institution of Washington, Publication No. 531 (Washington, 1941).

Stephens, John L., *Incidents of Travel in Yucatán*, 2 vols. (New York, 1843).

Thompson, J. Eric S., *Maya Hieroglyphic Writing*, Carnegie Institution of Washington, Publication No. 589 (Washington, 1950).

————— , *Maya History and Religion* (Norman, 1970).

————— , "The Moon Goddess in Middle America, with Notes on related Deities," Carnegie Institution of Washington, Publication No. 509, Contribution No. 29 (Washington, 1939).

————— , "Maya Chronology: the Correlation Question," Carnegie Institution of Washington, Publication No. 456, Contribution No. 14 (Washington, 1935).

————— , *Maya Hieroglyphs without Tears* (London, 1972).

————— , *A Catalog of Maya Hieroglyphs* (Norman, 1962).

Tozzer, A. M., "Chichen Itza and its Cenote of Sacrifice," *Memoirs of the Peabody Museum of Archaeology and Ethnology*, Harvard University, vols. XI-XII (1957).

————— , *see* Landa, Diego de.

Von Hagen, V. W., *The Aztec and Maya Papaermakers* (New York, 1943).

Wagner, H. R., *The Discovery of Yucatán by Francisco Hernández de Córdoba*. Documents and Narratives concerning the Discovery and Conquest of Latin America. New Series, No. 1 (Berkeley, 1942).

West, Robert C., "Surface Configuration and associated Geology of Middle America," *Handbook of Middle American Indians*, (Texas, 1965) vol. 1, pp. 33-83.

Willey, Gordon R., and William R. Bullard, Jr., "Prehistoric Settlement Patterns in the Maya Lowlands," *Handbook of Middle American Indians*, (Texas, 1965) vol. 2, pt. 1, pp. 360-377.

Index

185

189